MIRA
ME

CW00550147

NIKHIL NAZ is an award-winning sports journalist and presenter. The last 17 years have seen him travel across the globe to cover some of the biggest sporting events, including the ICC Cricket World Cups, the FIFA World Cup and the summer Olympic Games. *Miracle Men* marks his debut as an author.

MIRACLE MEN

THE GREATEST UNDERDOG STORY IN CRICKET

NIKHIL NAZ

hachette INDIA

First published in 2019 by Hachette India
(Registered name: Hachette Book Publishing India Pvt. Ltd)
An Hachette UK company
www.hachetteindia.com

1

ISBN 978-93-88322-23-2

Hachette Book Publishing India Pvt. Ltd
4th & 5th Floors, Corporate Centre
Plot No. 94, Sector 44, Gurugram - 122003, India

Typeset in Arno Pro 11.5/15.3
by Manmohan Kumar, Delhi

Printed and bound in India by
Manipal Technologies Limited, Manipal

To my late father, Col. Nawal Naz, the man who introduced me to sports and storytelling – two passions that enabled me to write this book

The 1983 Indian Cricket Team

Standing (L–R) : P.R. Man Singh, Yashpal Sharma, Krishnamachari Srikkanth, Balwinder Singh Sandhu, Ravi Shastri, Sandeep Patil, Roger Binny, Kirti Azad, Sunil Valson

Sitting (L–R) : Dilip Vengsarkar, Syed Krimani, Kapil Dev, Mohinder Amarnath, Sunil Gavaskar, Madan Lal

Contents

Contents

1

Cricket Crush

25 June 1983, Bombay, India

Through the curly strands of hair that are falling over his eyes, he can partially see a boy, as young as himself, scrawny, in shorts and a T-shirt, running towards him from a distance of about 28 yards. Saccho takes a step back, straightens his back and holds out his right hand signalling him to stop. The boy charging in obliges. Saccho now dips the same right hand into the pocket of his hip-hugging shorts and pulls out a headband. A red headband. Pushing his sweaty mop back, he places the headband in its position, bends down and taps his bat on the concrete floor as the scrawny lad approaches him all over again. Four taps of the bat later, the ball, which left the hands of his bony mate a microsecond ago, is travelling towards the fourth floor of the adjoining building. Crashing through the window glass, it bounces on a dusty mattress on the floor, ricochets off a black trophy at the corner of the study table – the trophy now dislodged – before settling down on the book shelf, stuck in the gap between the wooden frame and the corner-most book: *Shantata! Court Chalu Aahe*, by Vijay Tendulkar – the most famous Tendulkar in the country.

Saccho and his friends have promptly dispersed from their makeshift cricket pitch inside the compounds of Sahitya Sahawas. All seven of them, hiding behind a blue Fiat parked on the side, are looking at the broken window of the fourth-floor flat nervously.

The 47-year-old occupant of the flat comes out of his nearly bare kitchen, effortlessly pulls out the rubber ball, and throws it out through the jagged gap in the window that the ball had created just a few seconds ago. He then picks up the trophy – a sculpted black lady – and places it back on the table. The placard at the bottom reads: Filmfare Best Dialogue – Satyadev Dubey, *Junoon* (1980).

Satyadev came to Bombay three decades ago from Bilaspur, with the dream of becoming a cricketer. He moved into Sahitya Sahawas – a residential society that houses some of the finest writers and poets of Marathi and Hindi literature – some nine years ago. In that time, he wrote and directed a range of award-winning plays and films. Adapting Vijay Tendulkar's iconic play *Shantata! Court Chalu Aahe* into a full-length Marathi feature film remains Satyadev's most satisfying accomplishment. If only he could write half as well as Mr Tendulkar, he wishes every day.

His unrealized dream of becoming a famous cricketer doesn't bother him at all any more. He lives in the hope of Gen Next making it big in the game. Hence, the tossing back of the ball.

Saccho is now stretching his leading leg to the pitch of the ball. But the ball deviates at the last second – courtesy the protuberance on the cement grill covering the underground drain. But that's no matter for Saccho – he transfers his body weight on to his muscular, bulging left thigh and brings the bat down in a flash; the ball is sailing towards the colony gate.

Crash!

The white lamp atop one of the two pillars holding the black iron gates at the entrance of Sahitya Sahawas is lying shattered on the tarmac. This time the notorious bunch of 10-year-olds aren't hiding. They've decided to run into their respective houses instead. It's only a matter of time before Laxman Kaka, the society's watchman, comes chasing after them with a large bamboo stick in hand.

That's the end of the day's play for Saccho and gang. Their makeshift cricket ground, in the gap between two 17-year-old residential buildings, has seen the last of the day's cricket action. Laxman Kaka has plonked himself down on a wooden stool right in the middle of their pitch. But it's a Saturday afternoon. School is off. And four good hours of sunlight still remain. There's no way cricket-crazy Saccho is going to let that go waste. In his mind, four hours equals 500 balls of either batting or bowling.

The central park of Sahitya Sahawas, surrounded by trees on three sides that don't allow cricket balls to barge into houses uninvited, is still witnessing cricket action, though. Unfortunately, it's out of bounds for Saccho and his mates. This is big-boy territory. Playground to Saccho's elder brother and friends. Sixteen years and upwards. There are no soft rubber balls here. The white hard MRI ball is the bowler's weapon of choice. Bowlers who can bowl with a run-up as long as they desire and not restricted to just six yards because that's all that a pitch in the middle of two residential buildings can afford.

Saccho sits on the parapet, looking expectantly at the big boys play. 'Will today be the day I get invited?' he wonders. Just as he's wondered many a time before. Now for almost two years.

'Oye, McEnroe,' calls out the burly batsman who's been smashing the ball towards the tallest branches of the trees surrounding the ground.

Saccho responds with a wide smile. Red headband and curly mane intact.

'What are you doing sitting around here? Aren't you guys playing your own match?'

'No, Laxman Kaka won't let us.'

'You must have broken another window,' the wicketkeeper says confidently.

Junior McEnroe extends his lips into a half-smile. It has 'guilty' written all over it.

The big-boy group lets out a collective laugh.

For the next 15 minutes, Saccho's eyes are transfixed on his elder brother, Ajit, who's now fielding on the boundary close to him. The younger sibling hasn't said a word. He doesn't need to. His puppy-dog eyes are enough for Ajit to know what he desires.

'Listen, you are still too small to play with a hard ball, and against such fast bowlers. When I think you're good enough, I'll be the first one to let you in.'

'But...'

'Let's leave this discussion for another day. This is the last over of the day anyway.'

'Why? It's only 3.'

'The World Cup final starts shortly, silly. We are all heading upstairs.'

The flat on the third floor of the Usha Kal building is overflowing with men of all ages: 28 of them stuffed together in the 200 square-foot living room. The 18-inch black-and-white TV screen is beaming live images from the Lord's Cricket Ground in London. Mr Gowariker, the owner of the flat, and his friends occupy the three sofas. Mr Gowariker's son, Avinash, and his friends – Sunil, Satyajit, Harshad, Ketan, Parag, Ramesh, Vivek and Junior McEnroe – are cramped up on the concrete floor, their heads tilting up in the direction of the TV screen. Ajit and his teenage friends are spread across the room, occupying the dining chairs, stools and the few available spots on the sofas.

Exactly a week ago, Sally Ride became the first American woman to travel into space on the space shuttle *Challenger*. In India, colour TV has just arrived. It's not yet made an appearance at Sahitya Sahawas, though. Mr Gowariker's black-and-white Dynora remains one of the rare home screens in all of Kala Nagar.

Gavaskar's dismissal early is met with a collective groan. Saccho can't fathom why. He looks around the room for a clue. No one is talking. 'Must be a very crucial blow,' he tells himself.

Srikkanth rocks back and hits Andy Roberts for a 6! Saccho doesn't need help to comprehend this. The gang of 10-year-olds on the floor break into an impromptu jig. 'No matter what the situation, this Srikkanth always plays like this,' Mr Gowariker explains to his friend.

Thirty-one overs later, India have lost four wickets, and Junior McEnroe his interest. The 60-over game is proving to be far too sluggish for a 10-year-old more accustomed to the quick-fire 10-over gully cricket format. This is not how he imagined his first international cricket match on TV would feel like.

'Hey... Where are you going? There are still 4 overs to go before lunch,' whispers Avinash as Saccho gets up.

'I'm going home. McEnroe's match is about to start.'

There aren't many takers for McEnroe in Sahitya Sahawas. Björn Borg is their hero.

Saccho stays in the same building as Avinash. A floor above. In a flat devoid of TV. He sits in front of a radio. Tennis shorts, T-shirt, red headband, et al. The commentator announces John McEnroe is leading 1-0 in the first set of his third-round match, versus compatriot Brad Gilbert.

The American brat is gunning for his second Wimbledon title. And this is as good a chance as any for him to repeat what he did two years ago. Björn Borg – his biggest rival and winner of 11 Grand Slams – retired just five months ago, aged 26.

McEnroe wins the first set 6-2. The second set is on.

But wait! What! The match has come to an abrupt halt. The fuzzy haired, red-headbanded tennis pro is being summoned by the chair umpire. Saccho is nervous. McEnroe has already had a near escape in his previous match against

Florin Segărceanu of Romania, where he was found guilty of abusing a ballboy, a line judge and the chair umpire, and then got fined. His fines for the year total $7200. That figure is likely to increase by the end of the day. He's now being warned for having screamed at a woman in the crowd. The match resumes. The 10-year-old boy sitting in Bombay breathes a sigh of relief.

6-2, 6-2, 6-2 is the final score. John McEnroe is through to the fourth round of Wimbledon. Junior McEnroe is through with his dinner.

'You watch, this target of 184 will be a cakewalk for this formidable West Indian batting line-up,' proclaims Ajit in a loud voice, as Saccho walks into the Gowariker living room once again and takes his place on the floor. His buttocks haven't even settled down before he hauls them up and moves vigorously. As do the rest of his friends. All thanks to Balwinder Singh Sandhu, who's sent the dangerous Gordon Greenidge's stump carting around.

Vivian Richards is allowing the dancing brigade at Sahitya Sahawas some rest. He's in ominous form. The Indian fielders have already made seven trips across the boundary rope. 'It's like he's batting on a different pitch to all the others,' Saccho hears his brother tell a friend. He wonders what it means, but chooses not to ask.

Richards's swinging bat has connected with the ball again. The ball is travelling miles up in the air. Will this be his eighth boundary of the match? The entire living room has its mouth wide open. Just as well. They needn't open it again when they have to scream. Kapil Dev has taken a stunning catch! India have their most-prized wicket.

The dancing is getting more vigorous with each West Indian wicket.

It's well past midnight. Suddenly, the most outlandish dance moves are rocking the third-floor flat of the Usha Kal building at Sahitya Sahawas society, of Kala Nagar area in Bandra East, Bombay. The last man, Michael Holding, is out! The West Indies have folded for 140 – 43 runs short of India's 183. Kapil and his 'devils' are the new World Champions. The greatest underdog story in cricket has been written. And this colony of writers is experiencing it all vicariously.

A carnival-like atmosphere has engulfed the entire city. Drums drumming, crackers cracking, and sweets in every mouth at every street corner.

After dancing and rejoicing on the streets, Saccho and gang have settled down on the benches of Nanda Deep – a community park down the road from their residential society – listening to Ajit and his friends recall some key moments from the final. It's 2 a.m. But there are no deadlines tonight.

'It was as if Viv Richards was batting on a different pitch from everyone else,' butts in Saccho, nervously. Unsure of whether what he has said fits the context of what his elder brother and friends are discussing. Plus, he feels guilty about copying his brother's line.

The members of the big-boy gang exchange glances – brows arched, eyes wider than usual – before carrying on with their conversation. Saccho doesn't know what to make of it.

26 June 1983

The central park at Sahitya Sahawas, surrounded by trees, and flanked by swings and slides on one side, is witnessing an engrossing cricket match amongst the 16-years-and-above of the society. A Sunday morning feature.

Saccho walks out of his building and is heading towards the adjoining one, Anandvan, to meet his friend Harshad.

'Oye, McEnroe!' shouts the bowler. 'You want to play with us? We are one guy short.'

Little Saccho grins, walks over to the centre and is given a bat to hold. He bends and takes a leg-stump guard. Sachin Ramesh Tendulkar is ready to face the next ball.

On the fourth floor of the building overlooking the park, Satyadev Dubey has settled in front of his study desk. He's beginning a new project – adapting a famous book into a TV series for Doordarshan. The book is *The Discovery of India*.

2

The Captaincy Conundrum

2 February 1983, Karachi, Pakistan

It's rest day in the sixth and final test between India and Pakistan, but for one member of the Indian team. Skipper Sunil Gavaskar's mind is hard at work. He's just learnt that his teammate Kapil Dev has cancelled his earlier plans to go to Delhi via the Wagah border, and instead asked to be booked on a flight to Bombay, along with the rest of the team. An astute man, Gavaskar can read the writing on the wall. As he paces up and down in the relatively large expanse of his hotel suite in Karachi, a privilege accorded only to the captain of the side even as the rest of the team is lodged in a twin-sharing arrangement, he recalls an informal meeting between national selector Bishan Singh Bedi, Kapil Dev and team manager Fatehsinghrao Gaekwad, on the sidelines of the fourth test of the series in Hyderabad – a test India lost by an innings and 119 runs. 'Why did the selector and manager speak to Kapil alone?' Gavaskar had pondered at the time. He now has the answer.

In Karachi, India are at the fag end of an arduous two-month tour of Pakistan. They've lost the one-day series 3-1 and are trailing 3-0 in the six-test series. Now, there are only two days of cricket left. An unsuccessful tour to Pakistan is the death knell for any Indian captain, Gavaskar knows. Why, he himself got his first shot at captaincy after Bishan Singh Bedi was sacked in 1978, following a 2-0 test defeat in Pakistan.

The vice captain, Gundappa Viswanath, too is having a forgettable run. His scores of 1, 24, 0, 53, 9, 0 and 27 have seen him getting dropped from the ongoing test. A selection committee meeting is scheduled in Bombay soon after the Karachi test. Kapil's last-minute change of plans can only mean one thing.

Four days later, Kapil Dev is announced as the new captain of the Indian cricket team. His first assignment: a five-test series against the formidable West Indies in 10 days' time.

The following Sunday, in his column for *Mid-Day*, Gavaskar writes: 'What is disappointing is the utter lack of courtesy and finesse with which the removal has come. Right from the time I started playing cricket at the test level to the present day, captains have been discarded as one would brush away some dust. Neither the Cricket Board Secretary nor the

Chairman of the Selection Committee calls to inform the deposed leader that he is no longer wanted as captain. Instead he has to learn about it from outside sources. What's the harm in one telephone call to the deposed captain?'

The telephone does ring at the Gavaskar household in Worli, Bombay. It's not a selector though. Nor a BCCI (Board of Control for Cricket in India) bigwig. Ayaz Memon, a greenhorn cricket writer at *Mid-Day*, who's just returned from his first-ever international cricket tour – the same ill-fated tour of Pakistan that has resulted in Gavaskar being sacked as captain – is chasing the juiciest story in Indian cricket at the moment: Kapil versus Gavaskar, Season Two.

Season One had taken place in 1979, when Pakistan came calling. Gavaskar was batting on 166 during the fifth test in Madras when he played a shot towards backward point off Imran Khan. He wanted a single, but Kapil at the non-striker's end declined. The next ball, Gavaskar's miss-hit of an Imran bouncer, landed safely in Iqbal Qasim's hands. The skipper returned to the dressing room an angry man. Ten minutes later, at teatime, during a heated exchange between the two, Gavaskar let Kapil know what he thought of his refusal to take that run. He was convinced that 'Kaps' could have handled the Imran bouncer better.

Today, four years later, Ayaz has called to know whether Gavaskar is hurt at being replaced as skipper by Kapil Dev – a player 10 years his junior. 'Not at all,' is Gavaskar's emphatic response. 'Contrary to what some people would like to believe, my relations with Kapil are excellent. He is a very honest person, who has nothing but the interest of the team at heart. Any time he asks me for anything, I will do it. I will certainly try to put in more than 100 per cent for him – like he did when I was captain.'

Ayaz has his scoop.

Yet, this is not the biggest story of the day. The finance minister of the country, Pranab Mukherjee's dog Daku has bitten the president of the newly formed Bharatiya Janata Party, Atal Bihari Vajpayee's finger when he was on a morning walk down Jantar Mantar. Daku attacked him when Vajpayee was trying to fend off the canine's onslaught on Lolly, his own Lhasa apso.

Kapil, though just 24, is already a superstar in international cricket. His impressive CV has him as the youngest cricketer to score 1000 runs and take 100 wickets in tests, all of which he accomplished at age 21. His exploits on the tour of England in 1982, where he outshone Ian Botham, had the English faithfuls comparing him to their favourite son, Beefy. Why, even during the recent hiding in Pakistan, the all-rounder scalped 24 wickets in six tests; overshadowed only by a rampaging Imran Khan, who finished with a total of 40.

But can a raw talent, from the hinterland, who speaks only the vernacular, be the cricket captain of a country where the sport itself is run by English speakers? The predominantly Bombay-based English press isn't sure. So, the inevitable is asked at the skipper's first press conference.

'Okay, get someone from Oxford then; he can speak and I can play,' Kapil retorts.

A day later, the brave face at the press conference has given way to brooding eyes, as Kapil sits in the comfort of his Chandigarh home, staring at the pale-yellow walls of his drawing room. He'd been appointed captain once before. Just five months ago, he led the Indian team against Sri Lanka in a one-off test match, after Gavaskar had been rested. But that had been an interim arrangement. This was the real deal.

Kapil had got wind of what was to come through some important channels during the Karachi test. He argued in favour of Gavaskar continuing as skipper to the decision-makers in the BCCI. The loss to Pakistan, he knew, was a result of the gulf in quality between the two sides and not down to a deficit in leadership. 'Even under these trying circumstances, Sunil remains a big influence on the side; motivating us to fight, no matter what the situation,' Kapil had said at the time.

A week later, sitting at home, he can see the larger picture. It wasn't about who the best man was for the job. It seldom is in Indian cricket. Players with powerful personalities were viewed as threats and cut to size on the first available opportunity by the cricket board. Currently, there is no bigger name than Gavaskar in Indian cricket.

'Divide and Rule,' mutters the little voice inside Kapil's head.

3

Born in Berbice

29 March 1983, Berbice, Guyana

It's been baptism by fire for captain Kapil so far. India trail 2-0 in the four-test series against the West Indies, with two matches still to go. They've also lost the first limited-overs match at Port of Spain, in what was a one-sided contest. The last few days have also seen the surrender of India's most wanted and fearsome dacoit, Phoolan Devi. The infamous 'Bandit Queen' is accused of terrorizing large sections of the population in two of the biggest states in the country. She has been charged with 40 crimes, including banditry and murder. Yet, the Indian team's performance on the current tour is the biggest contributor to the word 'surrender' in newsprint back home.

It's the Hindu festival of Holi today. There's a riot of colour all around. A sizeable population of Indian-origin Guyanese are celebrating. Sunil Gavaskar has a bird's-eye view of the festivities. But he's not watching. Sitting in a helicopter, eyes tightly shut, he is nervous. He'd rather be facing bouncers from Roberts and Holding than sit in this eggbeater – the most unnatural of all flying objects in his opinion; he prefers the more traditional and safe fixed-wing aircraft. Minutes later, it's touchdown, much to the relief of the Little Master, who emerges from the copter shell along with seven of his teammates. A second helicopter with eight other members of the squad follows.

Berbice, the venue for the second limited-overs match between India and the West Indies, is at the heart of the rich sugar belt of Guyana. Even so, there isn't a hotel good enough in the area to house the Indian and West Indian cricket teams. Which explains the airdrop. A swift return to Trinidad is planned soon after the match is over.

Unlike the rest of the Caribbean islands, which boast of emerald waters and white, sandy beaches, the sea in Guyana is brown. Fortuitously, the Albion Sports Complex in Guyana is also a sea of brown today. Thanks largely to the East-Indian population that stays in this small village of Albion, where 95 per cent of the people share an Indian heritage.

They don't get to see much top-quality cricket here. Even though the venue made its international debut five years ago, it's only the third occasion that the ground is hosting an international team, and the first time India are playing here. It's dry season in Guyana – the time to harvest the first sugar cane crop of the year. But for much of the sugar-farming community here, they'd rather be sipping on a drink made out of molasses than make the molasses itself, while watching the action unfold on the cricket field.

Fifteen thousand of them have turned up at the stadium. It's the only bald spot in a thick cover of coconut trees all around. Amongst them is Muhammad, a third-generation West Indian, whose ancestors came to Trinidad as bonded labourers, aboard British ships, more than 100 years ago, much like the rest of the Indian population in the Caribbean. Muhammad is a massive Sunil Gavaskar fan. Ever since he first saw him score 65* and 67* in the Port of Spain test of 1971, in what was the Little Master's test debut, he knew he had seen perfection. Today, he's made a day trip from Trinidad. Thanks in no small measure to the wager he won during the first test of the ongoing series at Queen's Park Oval.

Two weeks ago, Muhammad had placed a bet with a Trinidadian of African descent that Gavaskar would score more runs in the first innings than both the fabled West Indian opening pair of Greenidge and Haynes. Gavaskar was caught behind of Michael Holding on the first morning, for just 1. Muhammad honoured his bet and promptly paid up. As it turned out, the second day saw Balwinder Singh Sandhu dismiss Greenidge for nought, and soon Haynes was gone for a duck too. Muhammad missed the rest of the day's action and spent the afternoon tracing his friend in downtown Port of Spain. He finally found him in a bar, enjoying his spoils from a day ago. Muhammad, a teetotaller, didn't raise a toast that night, but the Trinidadian roti for dinner had never tasted better.

Today, he sits in one of the many temporary stands, with wooden benches, that have been erected to accommodate the spectators at the Albion Sports Complex. The overflows are happy standing. The breeze from the Atlantic – just a couple of kilometres away – along with a healthy dose of rum and Coke, is enough to keep them cool.

Clive Lloyd, though, is hot under the collar. One look at the pitch and he knows it's as slow as a Mohinder Amarnath bouncer. Not exactly the conditions his fast-bowling quartet of Holding, Roberts, Marshall and the debutant Winston Davis will cherish. Worse still, Guyana is home. A place he was born and raised. A place he learnt to play cricket as a 12-year-old by using discarded weight-training equipment. And the last place he expects to be offered unfavourable conditions. Even so, he has no hesitation in putting the visitors in. Confident his pace battery will mow down any batting attack, whatever the track.

It's the familiar sight of Sunil Gavaskar walking out to bat. There is a loud cheer from the large majority of Berbice

Indians. A few jeers too. Plausibly from the West Indian blacks, who haven't taken too kindly to the comments made about them by Gavaskar in his first book, *Sunny Days*. But soon, the focus shifts to the man accompanying Sunny.

Ravi Shastri has been entrusted with the task of opening the innings. A first for him in his nine-match one-day career.

Michael Holding is standing on top of his run-up. Sixty yards from Gavaskar. As he begins his Rolls-Royce–like run-up, Gavaskar can't stop the unsavoury memories from the last two months seeping through his usually uncluttered mind: the controversy following the release of *Sunny Days*; the references in it to the Jamaica test of 1976; the hostile bowling by Michael Holding, aided by a dodgy pitch at Sabina Park, posing serious danger to the life and limb of the Indian batsmen; five of his teammates declared 'absent hurt' for the fear of getting hit in the second innings; his complaint to umpire Ralph Gosein against the West Indian pacers for going overboard with their short-pitch bowling; his disgust at the behaviour of the crowds present at the stadium; how he called them a 'mob' in his autobiography all those years later – 'The way they shrieked and howled every time Holding bowled was positively horrible. They encouraged him with shouts of "Kill him Maan! Hit him Maan!" All proved beyond a shadow of doubt that these people still belonged to the jungles and forests, instead of a civilised country'; the extensive coverage of these uncomplimentary references in the Caribbean press right before the Indian team's departure for the tour; him nearly not making it to this tour, but for the last-minute decision that saw him reach on the eve of the first test, only to face another round of hostility from Messrs Holding, Garner, Roberts and Marshall – where else but at Sabina Park? – as he ducked, fended and scratched to a 20 in the face of serious rib-cage assault from the quartet, which made the legendary commentator Tony Cozier say from behind the mic – 'Surely this is not the Sunil we know. It's someone else. Someone disguised as Gavaskar!'; his struggles on this tour ever since, devoid of a single noteworthy innings in the two tests and one one-day match so far...

Michael Holding, now just 22 yards away, in one seamless motion lets the cherry go.

Gavaskar's bruised foot lands in line, the underutilized bat comes down in time, the swollen index finger on the top hand turns the handle fine. Cutting through all the cobwebs in his head... 4!

Holding's first 4 overs have seen him concede 28 runs.

The DJ isn't playing reggae any more. Bhojpuri lyrics mixed with Caribbean beats, or chutney music, is blaring from the speakers. The orange triangle flags are lending a real Hindu subcurrent to the event. Shastri is doing well to hold one end up. Gavaskar continues to score at 5 runs an over. As if channelizing his inner Rohan Kanhai – his favourite cricketer and idol, a man for all crises, known for his daring stroke play, especially in the face of adversity – who's sitting in the stands, fortuitously here, visiting his ailing mother who stays nearby, admiring each of Gavaskar's own daring strokes.

The two Bombaywallas put on 93, before Shastri is sent back by Malcolm Marshall for 30. Can Gavaskar become the first Indian to score a century in a limited-overs game? He's now just 10 runs short.

Soon, he's inches short of the crease. 117 balls later, he's walking back to the pavilion to a standing ovation, the Afro-Caribbean 'mob' included. 'Sunny Days are here again,' chimes Cozier on the mic.

Kapil promotes himself up the order and replaces Gavaskar once again, this time as batsman. At 152 for 2, the run rate is set to rise rapidly as Kapil sets about exploiting the one chink in the Windies armour – their inept spin department. He uses his gazelle-like feet to great effect, dancing down the pitch, especially against Gomes – and even against Rolls-Royce Holding – to hit seven balls across the turf to the fence, and three over it. Beyond the fence, the heckling from the partisan Indo-Caribbean crowd is rising. As is the frustration level of the home team made to feel like outsiders in their own backyard.

Somewhere between Kapil's lusty blows, Mohinder Amarnath has chipped in with 30 runs. Yashpal Sharma falls for 23 to Winston Davis – in the side for an injured Joel Garner – whose biggest achievement so far, before taking this wicket, has been to hold the joystick of the helicopter that airdropped him and his team to Berbice earlier in the day, thanks to an indulgent pilot.

Soon, Davis gets another chance to fly an object. His overpitched delivery has been sent skywards by Dilip Vengsarkar. Seconds later, the ball descends to hit the sight screen for a 6. Vengsarkar finishes unbeaten on 18 off 19 balls.

The scoreboard reads 282 for five in 47 overs. No team has scored more runs against the World Champions in their decade-long one-day history. Needless to say, this is also India's highest-ever one-day score.

The small dressing room of the Indian cricket team at the Albion Sports Club, with its bats, gloves, dirty-brown shirts and other cricket gear lying around, is overflowing with excitement. After a full month of being dominated, this is the first day on tour that seems to have gone their way. But the job is just halfway done. No one knows that better than the skipper: 'There are two teams in world cricket that can defend any total with their bowling – Pakistan and the West Indies. Then again, these are the same two teams that can also collapse under the pressure of chasing a big total. The pitch is still good for batting, so we have to be patient and let the game situation take its toll on them.'

Balwinder Singh Sandhu, the genial sardar from Bombay, has Gordon Greenidge struggling against his inswingers. Thanks in no small measure to Gavaskar, who recently advised Sandhu to make a subtle change in his action. Watching Sandhu in the nets, Gavaskar observed he sent a 'telegram' to the batsman by going wide of the crease every time he bowled an inswinger. Sandhu was quick to correct himself, and now, with no visible change in action, the batsman hadn't a clue which direction the ball would swing after pitching. Exhibit A: Gordon Greenidge.

Despite the tight bowling, a wicket still eludes Sandhu. Kapil comes over and says, 'Don't worry, a wicket will come. You just get me one of these openers and your job is done.' Next ball, Desmond Haynes is trapped leg before, bowled Sandhu. A few overs later, Kapil takes a fantastic catch off his own bowling to send the unusually docile Greenidge back into the hut. But he's hurt his thumb, forearm and chest in the process. With skipper Clive Lloyd out for 8, the hosts are tottering at 62 for 3.

The King – Vivian Alexander Richards – is still at the crease though. The sound of the ball hitting his bat is louder than the DJ's chutney beats. Viv is having the Indian bowlers for lunch. Soon, he's crossed his half-century. Then,

14 runs later, out of the blue, His Majesty's lavish spread is withdrawn from right under his nose. Madan Lal's delivery leaves his hand swinging away from the batsman and then nips back off the pitch to shatter the stumps. India have their most-prized scalp.

The rickety wooden benches in the makeshift stands can't take the weight of the foot-stomping, India-supporting, partisan crowd. A couple of rows cave under the pressure, much like the Windies batting. But none of the 20-odd fans who have fallen down want to leave the ground. Muhammed is one of them. He couldn't be bothered by a few cuts and bruises. Not when India is chugging along to a famous win.

The game isn't over though. India are facing a few more anxious moments. Jeff Dujon and Faoud Bacchus have made resolute half-centuries. The one-day champions are now just 90 short of the target.

Ravi Shastri has had a decent game so far, scoring 30 in his first attempt at opening the innings in a one-dayer. But it's about to get better.

His first spell of 8 overs of left-arm orthodox spin has accounted for three wickets, putting the hosts in an unorthodox position of losing a one-day match at home.

There's tension reported in the stands behind the square boundary. The turntables at the DJ console have come to a screeching halt. The music-less atmosphere is allowing the players in the middle to hear the vociferous squabble, laced with the choicest patois profanities. What was healthy banter a few minutes ago, has now turned into a slanging match between the two largest ethnicities of Guyana. The non-inclusion of Alvin Kallicharran has been a cause of vexation for Berbice Indians, who allege bias citing a team predominantly made up of Afro-Caribbean players. And the Windies's imminent loss is only making them more boisterous and the atmosphere more frenzied. The rising level of ethanol isn't helping the already tense situation. A minor scuffle breaks out, threatening to stall the match, which is already fighting fading light.

The end comes soon. Washing away any fears of abandonment with it. 255 for 9 is all the Windies can manage in their allotted quota of 47 overs. The 27-run win is India's first against the Caribbean islanders in one-day matches. It's also the first time a full-strength West Indies has been beaten at home in a one-dayer. Their only other loss in a limited-over game came against Australia five years ago. But that was a Windies team devoid of stars, all of whom had been taken in by the lure of big money promised by the Australian billionaire Kerry Packer and his 'World Series of Cricket'.

Many years later, Kapil Dev would write in his autobiography about one of the sweetest wins of his captaincy career, achieved, so to say, at the mouth of the Demerara, the most famous of sugar regions in the world: 'We found the chink in the West Indies' one-day armour. The day we knew they had an Achilles heel. The awe was gone. They were human. We had stopped selling ourselves short.'

The third edition of the cricket World Cup is 11 weeks away.

4

North-West Frontier

11 May 1983, New Delhi, India

Ayaz Memon sits in his office in suburban Bombay. There's a spring in his step after the hectic last few weeks. Apart from doing the graveyard shift at the sports desk of the *Mid-Day*, filing late-night updates on India's test matches in the West Indies, he's also helped his office organize and sell brochures – on the team's campaign for the forthcoming World Cup – to corporates in the country's financial capital, Bombay. All in an effort to raise money to go to England and cover his first global tournament. Ayaz, the zealous rookie, tasted blood during India's tour to Pakistan earlier in the year – his first-ever international cricket tour – and is now determined to cover the biggest tournament in cricket from the venue, rather than from the mundane confines of his office desk. *Mid-Day* is still in its embryonic stage, having begun its operations only four years ago, and doesn't have the necessary budget to fund the travel and lodging of its correspondent for the World Cup in England. Luckily for Ayaz, the brochures seemed to have done their job. His World Cup plans are all set to go! But that's not the only reason he's lively today. The Indian team for the World Cup is to be announced shortly and he's as excited as the rest of the country to know who the chosen 14 are.

A few kilometres from Ayaz's office sits captain Kapil Dev. He flew in a couple of hours ago from London and is awaiting his connecting flight to Delhi – the venue for the World Cup selection committee meeting. Kapil left for London from the Caribbean on 5 May – soon after the conclusion of the Antigua test, the fifth and last one of the largely forgettable tour of the West Indies – to honour his county cricket commitments with Northamptonshire. Less than a week later, he's decided to put his county stint on hold and be present at the World Cup selection meeting. In the VIP lounge of the Sahar airport, he sits in a pensive mood. On the table beside him lies a leading English daily, with its last page staring up at him. It carries an opinion piece by a well-known cricket writer who has his doubts about Kapil's ability to lead the side in a marquee tournament such as the World Cup.

Moments later, the airport announcement for his flight joggles him out of his brooding state. The north Indian born and bred Kapil realizes he's sitting in the western part of the country (a side which has perennially been at loggerheads with his own with regard to cricketing supremacy), a fact that had escaped his tired mind. Long flights tend to have that effect. He gets up from his comfortable sofa with a wry smile. The newspaper headline doesn't bother him any more. The Indian captain has the World Cup selection meeting to attend.

In a five-star hotel in India's national capital sit three wise men of Indian cricket. Ghulam Ahmed (61), Chandu Borde (49) and Bishan Bedi (37), all belong to different eras, but have a deep respect for each other. Both as cricketers and human beings. Two others, Pankaj Roy and Chandu Sarwate, selectors from the east and central zones, have given the meeting a miss. No one is blaming them. It's only a team for a one-day tournament, after all. No one ever misses a test selection meeting. Kapil, after his long journey – London–Bombay–Delhi, joins them. The fifth man in the five-star conference room is the convenor of the meeting, the BCCI secretary Anant Wagesh Kanmadikar.

Ahmed, the chairman of selectors, sits at the head of the table. Kanmadikar sits to his right, with his black briefcase lying on the table in front of him. To Kanmadikar's right is Borde – a distinctly striking personality with his broad forehead and frilly hairstyle; Bedi and Kapil sit opposite Kanmadikar and Borde respectively.

Before the selectors get down to their job, Kapil is asked for his inputs. The 24-year-old skipper – defying conventional logic – stresses on the need for a healthy mix of seniors and juniors. After the disastrous West Indies tour (one win in eight matches), wouldn't he want a complete overhaul, so he could start afresh? 'No,' is his short answer. He believes a lot of the seniors still have it in them to be part of his team. And a bunch of seven to eight youngsters should be a good-enough supporting cast. His other demand is for bowlers who can wield the bat. The idea is to have tailenders with a few first-class hundreds under their belt. 'It's a 60-over game and batting depth will be very crucial,' he stresses.

The selectors are on the same page. 'Horses for courses' is their motto of the day. Luckily, there aren't any injury concerns to be taken into consideration. All the talent available in the country is at their disposal. As the team begins to take shape, there emerges a distinct pattern in the type of players being selected. The press calls them 'bits and pieces' cricketers.

Mohinder Amarnath, one of the six all-rounders in the 14-member squad and who's had a fine run with the bat in the last seven to eight months, is unanimously elected vice captain.

There's a debate about Sandeep Patil. The flamboyant strokemaker from Bombay skipped the tour of the West Indies two months ago citing an injury. Though media reports suggest he skipped the tour in favour of a career in films, choosing to shoot his debut movie *Kabhie Ajnabi The* instead. His personal life is also on the rocks, with a divorce on the anvil. Considering the circumstances, should he be brought back? 'Not sure about his acting skills, but there's no doubting his credentials as a cricketer,' argues Borde, himself a former India captain. Ahmed, wearing thick, square-shaped spectacles, with an ashtray lying in front of him, nods in agreement. Patil's is the 13th name on the list.

The 14th and final spot is also up for grabs. Bedi suggests Sunil Valson's name. Valson doesn't have any international experience to show, but it's been a fine 1982–83 domestic season for the left-arm seamer. Add to that, he's playing for Seaham Park Cricket Club in Durham. 'Surely, his experience of playing in English conditions will come in handy,' argues Bedi. The genial Ahmed concurs again.

Kanmadikar signs the sheet with the 14 names on it and puts it in his leather briefcase. For the three sincere, unprejudiced men entrusted with the job of picking the team, and the two others in the room, this is the best possible team that can be conjured in all of India. The press, though, has other, more interesting angles, to explore.

Ayaz's hands are moving quicker over the typewriter today than Syed Kirmani's ever did while knocking the bails off the stumps. 'Valson getting selected is a sign of north's dominance in the selection process' is one of the many lines in his 800-word article about the Indian team selection, due to be out in print tomorrow.

Like *Mid-Day*, the other newspapers in Bombay have also dwelled on the fact that the players from the north zone have outnumbered the west in the World Cup squad: an aberration in Indian cricket. 'North pips West by 1' is the headline of a leading English daily, which highlights that six players from Delhi have been picked, while Bombay got only five.

But not all newspaper headlines on 12 May 1983 are obsessed with the north versus west debate. There's one article that talks about this being a healthy mix of north, west and south – the three most dominant regions in Indian cricket. 'A genuinely more representative Indian side than before,' it proclaims. Then there's a vernacular daily that says: '*Hindu, Muslim, Sikh, Issayi, hamari vishwa cup team mai pureh Bharat ki chavi hai samai*' – drawing attention to the presence of a Muslim, a Sikh, a Christian and Hindus in the team. A veiled attempt at shoring up communal harmony in the wake of the Nellie massacre – described as one of the worst pogroms since World War II. It saw over 2000 men, women and children brutally killed in central Assam, following Prime Minister Indira Gandhi's decision to give 4 million Bangladeshi immigrants the right to vote.

5

Off for a Holiday

12 May 1983

It's 4 a.m. in England when the phone rings in a compact one-bedroom apartment in the small market town of Burnley, in north England. Kirti Azad, half-asleep, picks up the receiver after eight long rings. He went to bed just two hours ago after a long night of pub-hopping in the nearby town of Manchester. The all-rounder from Delhi is in the UK as the lone professional for his club, Lowerhouse, which plays minor county cricket in the Lancashire league.

'This better be urgent,' he says to himself, before mumbling a 'hello' groggily into the receiver. 'Congratulations!' says the baritone at the other end. It's enough to force Kirti into sitting up in his bed, eyes wide awake. It's Bhagwat Jha Azad on the line. The sitting member of Parliament from Bhagalpur district in the eastern Indian state of Bihar, and a serving

Union minister of state for food and civil supplies. 'You have been selected to the Indian team for the World Cup. Congratulations, and all the best.' Before Kirti can muster a thank you, 'Here, talk to your mother,' says Azad senior and hands the phone over to his wife. 'Pappu *beta*, hope you are getting good food to eat…' Pappu's mind isn't registering a thing that's being spoken over the phone any more, even as Mrs Azad continues to inquire about her son's health. The body's state of arousal has kicked the hangover away. Moments after hanging up, he's out of his bed and swinging his bat. He can picture the ball racing past the boundary.

At the break of dawn, 6 a.m. to be precise, Kirti makes a call to Durham. Sunil Valson is up and about, getting ready to head out for a game for his club, Seaham Park. 'World Cup team?' He can't believe what Kirti is telling him. Later in the day, the left-arm pacer bowls a yard quicker than he's ever bowled before. High adrenaline levels are doing their thing.

The phone call that brings Kirti's excitement levels back to normal comes at 11 a.m. Kapil Dev, his skipper, is glad to have him as part of his team. Kirti, on his part, thanks his captain for granting him a 'free holiday'. 'It's not like we are going to win anything much, right?' Kapil isn't too pleased with Kirti's insouciant remark. His effervescent tone turns severe. 'No, we will fight. No matter the team or the result.' Kirti, on this occasion, decides it's best he bite his tongue.

Meanwhile, another phone call is made simultaneously. Only this one is from the UK to India.

'Do you want to go for your second honeymoon, Cheeka?' This is Sunil Gavaskar, who too is playing county cricket in England, asking Krishnamachari Srikkanth after the latter's selection to the World Cup squad. Srikkanth has just returned from his honeymoon in Sri Lanka. But who would ever let slip the opportunity for another holiday with his wife? Especially when it is all paid for. Surely, his wife, Vidya, would love it. A series of exhibition games are planned between a bunch of Indian cricketers and Indian expats in the US, organized by the United States Cricket Association, explains Gavaskar. The plan is to play the World Cup group games, and then, after the Indian team is knocked out of the tournament, watch the semis and finals from the sidelines. Post that, head to America for a cricket-cum-holiday trip. The proposition is tempting and it doesn't take long for Cheeka to answer in the affirmative. Sunny and Cheeka aren't the only ones going. Syed Kirmani, Roger Binny, Sandeep Patil, Yashpal Sharma and Balwinder Singh Sandhu are also expected to join the party.

Meanwhile, there are three other Indian cricketers playing professional cricket in England at the moment – Mohinder Amarnath, Ravi Shastri and Dilip Vengsarkar. Dilip and Ravi are heading to India in a few days, and plan to return to England with the rest of the team. Amarnath, who's based in

Lancashire, ties up with Kirti, who stays only a few miles away, to go together straight to London's West Moreland hotel once the team arrives on 1 June.

Sandeep Patil is ecstatic about finding his way back into the team. There is trouble in his paradise all right, but he's determined not to let this opportunity go by. He puts in a request with the BCCI secretary Kanmadikar to be allowed to go to London as soon as possible so that he can get acclimatized to the conditions. Patil plans to practise with the London Edmonton Club – whom he plays for in England. The BCCI's approval is instant.

30 May 1983, Bombay

For the BCCI to hold a farewell reception when an Indian team departs for a test tour is the norm. It's an occasion to wish the touring party the best of luck for the battles ahead. But this isn't a test series. Neither is it a tour where much is expected of the travelling team. Hence, there's no jamboree planned.

Before the team leaves for the Bombay international airport, noted BCCI administrator and former first-class cricketer Raj Singh Dungarpur is asked to interview the captain by the national broadcaster Doordarshan. 'So, young man, looking forward to your next assignment?' he asks. 'No,' pat comes the reply from Kapil. A bit taken aback with the answer, Dungarpur tries again. 'What? You aren't looking forward to the World Cup?' 'I don't want to look forward. I like to stay in the present,' says Kapil nonchalantly. Dungarpur lets out a loud guffaw. The chuckle from the cameraman results in the frame losing focus. The interview continues after a brief pause. It's now in Hindi.

At the airport, the 10 travelling members of the Indian team – four others are already in England playing professionally – are not being allowed to board the flight to London. Evidently, the comedy for the day isn't over. Formal and private clothes, coupled with all the cricket equipment, mean that the team's baggage is way over the prescribed weight limit. P.R. Man Singh, the bespectacled manager of the Indian team, and a former cricketer from Hyderabad, tries to reason with the airline staff. 'This is the Indian national cricket team going to England to play the World Cup. Could you please make an exception?' The ground staff is having none of it. The duty manager is called. He spells out exactly what his crew has been saying for the past half an hour: 'Pay the excess baggage fee or leave a few bags behind.' The trouble is, aside from not hosting a farewell, the BCCI hasn't fared well in giving the manager enough currency to pay for miscellaneous expenses. Even the billboards showing off the faces of Gavaskar and Kapil, which sell a thousand products, aren't cutting the mustard. The airline crew refuses to budge.

Despite the gravity of the situation – a World Cup team missing their scheduled flight; a first in the history of Indian cricket – the 44-year old manager is unperturbed. The equanimity helps. Moments later, he comes up with a smart piece of legerdemain. The team is now on its way, cruising at 30,000 feet above sea level. Just as the airline duty manager tucks away a letter titled 'Undertaking' into the top drawer of his desk. The letter, on the BCCI's letterhead, states that the excess baggage amount will be paid within 24 hours by the BCCI office in Bombay. Signed – P.R. Man Singh, Manager, Indian Cricket Team.

Two days later, it's Ayaz's turn to leave for London. Thankfully for him, going to England doesn't require a visa for an Indian national. Saving him all the trouble he had to face while going to Pakistan to cover cricket some time ago – the visa itself had taken more than a month to come through. But unlike the Indian team, all the excess baggage he's carrying is firmly embedded in his head. Enid Blyton in early school. Doyle, Agatha Christie, Charles Dickens and Shakespeare during adolescence and adulthood. *Wisden*, A.A. Thomson and Neville Cardus in his professional years… England to Ayaz was the promised land. Going there for the first time is no less than a pilgrimage.

As he fastens his seat belt and settles down for the nine-hour journey on the Singapore airlines flight, the young scribe's mind is on overdrive just thinking about everything he had to see and do in England. Scones, Yorkshire pudding, Trafalgar Square, Fleet Street, Buckingham Palace are just some of the things and places he's read and heard of. He can't wait to experience it all.

6

Fresh off the Boat

1 June 1983, London, United Kingdom

Ten nattily dressed members of the Indian cricket team alight from the big vessel that's brought them to London. Uniformly dressed in navy blue three-piece suits, white shirts and neckties. The BCCI's coat of arms conspicuous by its absence on the jacket pocket. But shopping bags with 'Dubai Duty Free' in bold red letters are eye-catching. Presumably, the stopover in the Gulf nation was well utilized.

It's a warm day in London. Half the squad have stuffed their waistcoats back into their brown leather handbags. Gavaskar's has the Thums Up logo on it – he is one of the rare cricketers with an endorsement deal. They are expecting an unusually warm summer this season, the immigration officer at the Heathrow airport informs them, before going on to ask Mohinder Amarnath whether they were sure they've been invited to the World Cup considering their dismal record at the last edition, where Amarnath was a participant. Turns out, the immigration official isn't just a soothsayer, but a student of history too. Only, he's picked the wrong guy to sledge. Amarnath is one of those gutsy men in cricket who doesn't let even the most proficient of sledgers affect him. The likes of Javed Miandad have tried, and failed. So, the man with the stamp stands no chance of leaving an imprint on Amarnath's uncluttered mind. Much like the Indian cricket team, which, despite its striking appearance, goes largely unnoticed at the airport. There are no media cameras and reporters to receive or even grill them.

The World Cup on the whole is a bit low-key. Paling in comparison to the attention that Prime Minister Margaret Thatcher enjoys at the moment. She has emerged as one of the few political leaders to have an 'ism' attached to her name. Tax cuts, low inflation, free market and nationalism are being collectively called Thatcherism. The right-wing leader, the daughter of a grocer, is running the country like a frugal housewife. A style that has seen her emerge as the undisputed queen bee.

As is the norm, the newsprint across the island is dedicated to the happenings in the palace of Westminster. Today, it is even more so. It's election season – nine days before the vote. The opinion poll shows the Conservatives, led by Iron

Lady Thatcher, are all set to be re-elected by a landslide. The sport pages have had to bear the brunt of the rising political stock. The *Times* has only two pages of sport today, unlike the regular dose of four. One entire page has been reserved for top-flight English football. Half of the next page features Teenoso, an American-bred, British-trained racehorse, who's just won the Epsom Derby – Britain's richest horse race. The remaining half has cricket news, divided into two articles. The first one features the scorecard of Zimbabwe beating a team of minor counties in a warm-up game ahead of the World Cup. The same piece carries a quote from the Zimbabwe batsman Ali Shah, who is of the opinion that India are the weakest team in their group: a group featuring the West Indies, Australia and India, besides Zimbabwe. This, coming from a member of a team making its World Cup debut.

The other article is a brief preview of the World Cup tournament on the whole. It has listed the West Indies, Pakistan, Australia and New Zealand as the favourites to reach the semi-finals. Sitting in the team bus, holding the *Times* in his hand, Syed Kirmani is reading both these cricket items out loud. The entire team is all ears as they head to their hotel from the airport.

The Westmorland Hotel is right opposite the 'Home of Cricket', the Lord's Cricket Ground, and overlooks the practice pitches located behind the main playing area. In fact, if your room is anywhere between the seventh and the eleventh floors, you can spot which way the ball is likely to seam – just by looking at the way the bowler is gripping it. The Indian team members are allotted their rooms. The ones in England – Patil, Amarnath, Azad and Valson – have already checked in. Two to a room is the norm. With the exception of the captain and the manager. They've got a room for themselves. Albeit rather small ones. Small rooms are standard in hotels across England. In stark contrast to the spacious ones in five-star hotels back home. They don't have much of a view either. The higher floors have already been occupied by the teams that arrived before them – Sri Lanka, Australia, Pakistan, New Zealand and Zimbabwe. The traffic roundabout at St John's Wood and the frieze featuring cricketers with the Ashes urn at the south-east corner of the Lord's are what they will have to wake up to for the next few days.

A 15-minute walk from Westmorland is Baker Street. It's Wednesday night. The offices are empty; the stores are shut. It's well past the working hours. Pubs are filled to the brim. The street smells foul. A result of malt, hops and yeast blending with stone and sand. Empty beer cans lie around.

The corner shop near 221B, the London residence of Sherlock Holmes, is an aberration. It's open. 'Jinhe naaz hai Hind par', a classic from Guru Dutt's 1957, multiple award–winning film Pyaasa, sung by the legendary Mohammed Rafi, is playing softly in the background. Jiten Bhai Parekh, the owner of the shop, is sipping hot water with a single teabag immersed in it, trying his best to keep his eyes open. He's been up since 6 a.m. Been at his shop since 8 a.m. Business isn't brisk at this hour. But every penny counts. He's the only earning member of a family of four. Living in England isn't cheap. He didn't know that when he migrated from India 35 years ago. At 20, he was young and naive. But what other option did he have? A high-school degree wasn't going to help him earn a comfortable living in newly independent India. Hell, even if he had been adequately educated, India was hardly the place for him to realize his dreams: that of owning a house, a fancy shop and a car. The economy of the country had been left paralysed after almost 200 years of British rule. The material deprivation triggered an exodus from India, and Britain emerged as the land of promise. The British Nationality Act of 1948 – the year Jiten Bhai migrated – enabled migration from Commonwealth countries with very limited conditions. Jiten Bhai made best of this and moved lock, stock and barrel. Now, 35 year later, he is living in a mortgaged apartment and driving his family around in a Yugo 45. The 45 horses of the supermini hatchback find it impossible to go past the 30 miles per hour mark on the speedometer the day all four Parekhs are on board.

A gang of four enters the shop. One of them, clean shaven and with neatly combed hair, picks up a packet of cigarettes lying near the cash register. The other, wearing a hoodie, pops opens a can of cola from the fridge. The third is too drunk to do anything. He is barely able to stand. His eyes, from behind his ruffled hair falling on his forehead, are trained on the shop's ceiling. The biggest guy out of the four, sporting a Garibaldi and a tonsured head, turns off the stereo mode of the music system playing the Rafi song and puts it on radio mode. '*Every breath you take*' by The Police is playing on the local FM. The bully turns the volume up. It's the number one track on the UK's Top 40 charts this week. Jiten Bhai is gobsmacked by the audacity of the lad. He's about to unleash his entire vocabulary of English profanity – a sum total of three words – before the ice-cold stare from the bare-head forces him to gulp down his words. Then, the four walk out of the store without paying for the items they've picked up. Jiten Bhai can't hold himself any longer. He walks behind them and demands they pay for what they've taken. Before he can finish his sentence, the man-mountain grabs hold of his throat, lifts him off his feet, and throws him back into the shop. All in one motion. He then re-enters the shop, opens the cash register and dips his hands in. No sooner has Jiten Bhai gotten up to stop him, the scrawny teen with the hoodie lands a punch on his left cheek. Blackout! 'Go home, you fucking Paki,' says the well-turned-out, clean-shaven brat.

Seconds later, the gang walks away with cash stuffed in their pockets. There are a few passers-by. No one stops to inquire if Jiten Bhai is okay. Cold sandwiches, broken coffee bottles, packets of biscuits and crushed toiletries are lying on the floor. So too is the middle-aged owner of the shop. Two of the biggest racks in the store have been felled. A fresh song comes on the radio. The track is called 'Whitepower', a recently released single by the white supremacist rock band Skrewdriver:

I stand watch my country, going down the drain
We are all at fault, we are all to blame
We're letting them takeover, we just let 'em come
Once we had an Empire, and now we've got a slum

7

A Cold Warm-up

3 June 1983

The Indian team is in Woodside, Watford. A half-hour drive from central London. It's a picturesque setting for a game of cricket. White-coloured, single-floor dressing rooms at square leg. A two-storeyed clubhouse made of red bricks at midwicket. A few residential houses further back. The rest of the field is surrounded by trees. It's home to the Watford Town Cricket Club. It's only the second time this ground is hosting an international team. Two years ago, Sri Lanka played a practice match against Middlesex here. Today, India are taking on New Zealand in a warm-up game ahead of the Prudential World Cup. The main reason this amateur club's ground was selected for a high-profile game such as this is the quality of the pitch.

The Kiwis bat first. It's a brisk start. The top order of Glenn Turner, Bruce Edgar and Martin Crowe send the Indian fielders on a leather hunt. Some balls hit the rooftops of neighbouring houses. It's a local ground all right, but by no means small. If anything, some of the boundaries are bigger than a few international venues in England. The middle and lower order suffer a minor collapse. But the 43, 41 and 34 by Turner, Edgar and Crowe respectively, help put 246 on the board before the entire team is dismissed inside the quota of 55 overs.

The hammering at the hands of the Kiwi batsmen doesn't worry the Indians as much as what has been served for lunch. Roasted chicken, shepherd's pie and jacket potatoes aren't exactly what they'd call appetizing. Especially the vegetarians in the team. The jacket potatoes are just about edible. After all, the Indian palate has always had a hostile relationship with anything that's bereft of sugar and spice.

Manager Man Singh is running helter-skelter, trying to arrange for some Indian food. His efforts bear no fruit. There's nothing in the vicinity. He comes in contact with an Indian fan though. Mintu Bhatia and his friends Kulwant Singh and Saran Gill are amongst the handful of Indians who've come to watch the team in action. Mintu owns an Indian restaurant in Southall. On hearing of the quandary that the manager is in, he promptly orders his staff to send over some food. 'It will be here in an hour,' Mintu tells Man Singh. But for now, the Indian stars will have to make do with potatoes, bread and biscuits.

The starch and baked goods fail to fuel. 212 is all that the Indian batting line-up can manage. Lance Cairns gets three, Ewen Chatfield and Evan Gray two wickets apiece. New Zealand win by a comfortable margin of 34 runs.

However, there's no despondency in the Indian dressing room. The food from Mintu's restaurant has arrived. Everyone is digging in. The butter chicken is over even before half the team can sample it. Not to worry, there is plenty of kadhai paneer and dal makhani to devour. It's only a practice game, after all.

4 June 1983

It's another day, another obscure, yet beautiful, cricket ground, and another warm-up match for India. This time, they are 40 miles to the west of central London, in the affluent neighbourhood of Princes Risborough. Unlike the rich neighbourhood, India's opponents have meagre resources at their disposal. It's a team made up of plumbers, farmers and salesmen. Batting first, it's tough labour for the semi-professionals against the more accomplished team. A measly 154 is all they can manage in the allotted 50 overs. Ravi Shastri picks up three out of the six minor county's wickets to fall. Lunch is a lavish spread, courtesy Mintu Bhatia once again. There's added variety this time in the form of theplas and churmuras, brought over by a few Gujarati fans who've come to watch.

India bat after a sumptuous lunch. Only to make a meal of it. Kris Srikkanth with 28 is the highest scorer. India is all out for 135 – 19 runs short, with 38 balls to spare. The unknown S.G. Plumb and P.G. Garner have shared seven wickets between them. This Indian team is in deep water – it's taken a bunch of plumbers and farmers for the cricket world to know.

But the warm-up defeats fail to whisk away the joviality of the Indian team. The mood is as bright as ever as they pack their bags to go back to London. A bunch of volunteers are waiting by the team bus. They are conducting an on-the-spot blood donation camp. A couple of them request Sandeep Patil. The quintessential prankster directs them to Yashpal Sharma, saying, 'His blood is the healthiest because it's made up of almonds.' A jibe at Yashpal's fondness for eating badams. Yashpal, a strongly built Punjabi, is a dedicated cricketer. He has many endearing qualities, but a sense of humour isn't one of them. Easily provoked, he picks up his bat and charges towards Sandeep. A timely intervention from Balwinder Singh Sandhu ensures that both escape without serious injuries. Following the fracas, the mood during the journey is sombre. Allowing for players to contemplate on their performances so far.

6 June 1983

Five thousand miles away from India, but it feels like home. A large number of British Indians have turned up for the game today. Unsurprising, since 37 per cent of Leicester county residents are of Asian origin. Indians predominantly, followed by Pakistanis and Bangladeshis. Fans apart, a cricket royalty is in attendance. Sir Garfield Sobers is sitting in the Sri Lankan camp. The islanders have managed to poach arguably the greatest to have ever played the sport to coach them through the tournament.

For the third time in a row, Kapil's men are bowling first. It's a green pitch that is expected to help India's seam bowlers. The first 60 overs though paint a very different picture. The Sri Lankan batsmen make merry. Young Don Kuruppu smashes 101, living up to the name he shares with the legendary Don Bradman. The experienced Roy Dias stitches together a fine 80. 265 for 4 is looking like a formidable target. And Grace Road isn't a small ground either. The straight boundaries are 60 metres, whilst the rope square off the wicket is at 76 metres. Larger than most county grounds around England.

The Indian openers are out early, even before they can test how long the boundaries are. But, for the muscular arms of Yashpal, fed on a healthy diet of almonds, nothing seems out of reach this afternoon. The Ludhiana resident smashes a fine 90. Kapil gives him company and notches up a gritty 64*. India romp home with five wickets to spare.

As Kapil walks back to the pavilion, he notices a Sikh gentleman going through his kitbag. He hasn't a clue who he is. The only sardar in the team is Balwinder Singh Sandhu. And this certainly isn't him. Kapil grabs hold of the intruder's hand and demands he explain his action. Only for the entire dressing room to erupt into laughter. Kapil is bemused. 'What's funny?' he thunders. Five seconds of pin-drop silence later, the sardar removes his turban and a bald head emerges. It's Syed Kirmani! The team's ever-jovial wicketkeeper.

As the crowds begin to leave, a local journalist approaches Sir Sobers to know his thoughts on the Indian team. 'These guys might be the underdogs, but watch out for them in the World Cup.'

8

London Eye

8 June 1983, London

Ayaz has settled in at the Indian YMCA hostel. He's on a shoestring budget. A bunk bed in the heart of London suits him just fine. The last four days have been surreal. Imagine, pushing a currency bill into a vent and out pops a chocolate bar of your choice. Vending machines are what they call this magic box here, the bug-eyed Ayaz has learnt. And then, the travel pass that allows him to get on any mode of public transport he likes – bus, train – 'What a luxury,' he's telling himself. What's more, no one is being hauled up for not producing a ticket. It's a whole new world. The overcrowded Bombay local train is a thousand miles away.

In all of this, Ayaz hasn't found the time to visit a cricket ground. The real reason he is here. The same is the case with the five other Indian journalists who have come here to cover the World Cup. They too have not covered even one of India's practice matches so far. Not much is known back home about India's performances thus far. That they've lost three out of the four warm-up matches (India lost to Sri Lanka by 16 runs in their last game, played at Chalvey Road, Slough – a day after they beat them in Leicester) has gone largely unnoticed in India.

The Indian team is at the Buckingham Palace. So are the seven other teams playing the World Cup. The Queen's residence is the venue for the customary reception ahead of the marquee tournament. The best cricketing talent from across the globe, all under one roof. All wearing their team blazers. Except two teams. Pakistan have donned beige suits with green ties, minus the team crest on their left breasts. And the English players are wearing suits of their own choice. It's olive for Bob Willis, light grey for David Gower, dark grey for Ian Botham, and so on. The Indians have on their traditional navy-blue jackets, white shirts and dark grey bell-bottoms. Kirti Azad is the only one wearing a black shirt instead of white. Much to the amusement of the other teams. A dark shirt under a suit is taboo in fashion-conscious England. Almost illegal, in fact. Kirti couldn't care less. He reckons he's the cat's pajamas.

For most, this is the first time they are meeting the Queen of England, 57-year-old Elizabeth II. The Belgian glass chandelier in the central hall is imposing enough, let alone the honour of shaking hands with the Queen.

Each player is announced in by a Grenadier Guard, wearing his traditional bearskin and red tunic. The usually phlegmatic queen's guard is having trouble pronouncing Indian names. 'Modern' Lal, Syed 'Kriminali' and 'Chris Sri-Can't' are introduced. Nervously, they, along with 11 other teammates, shake hands with the royalty. Champagne and strawberries follow. Gavaskar and Binny are savouring the bubbly. Yashpal is missing his tea. The history student in Azad wants to visit the Gwalior suite and the Nizam of Hyderabad hall. He's heard that parts of the Buckingham Palace are dedicated to Indian royalty. As the son of a powerful politician and as an international cricketer, he enjoys free access to most places in India. Not here. He can't go beyond the hall he finds himself in, he's promptly told. His sense of entitlement takes a beating.

It's the eve of the third edition of the Cricket World Cup. All eight teams are in action tomorrow, playing their first match of the tournament simultaneously. The Indian team is off to Manchester. Sprawled in their cosy team bus. A 40-seater luxury coach, catering to only 14 occupants. There is a video player on board, reclining seats and a water closet at the back. This is going to be home for the next two weeks. A place they are likely to spend more time in – travelling around the island – than in any hotel room in England. The senior pros – Gavaskar, Kapil, Amarnath, Kirmani and Vengsarkar – have made themselves comfortable in the front rows. The reticent bunch of Madan Lal, Binny, Yashpal and Valson settle in the middle. And the mischievous pack of Patil, Azad, Sandhu, Shastri and Cheeka occupy the back of the bus – backbenchers, if you please.

There are less than 24 hours to go before Kapil's Devils take the field for their first match of the tournament. It's the mighty Windies first up: the defending World Champions. It's a four-hour drive to Manchester from London. Both teams are scheduled to reach the city on the eve of the match. There's no time for a practice session at the venue. Hell, there's no time for even a team meeting! For plans and strategies, this bus ride will have to do.

The skipper begins with a rhetorical question: 'We beat them in Berbice just two months back, remember? Why we can't do it again?' A couple of backbenchers realize Kapil is talking; they promptly press pause on their Walkmans and remove their headphones. 'I just want our bowlers to bowl a stump-to-stump line, and we win.' The entire team is now listening in rapt attention. Kapil continues, 'Gentlemen, I don't need to tell everyone about their responsibilities. I'm lucky to have seven experienced players by my side and you are all going to guide me for the next few days.'

Gavaskar is next. 'The key to beating the West Indies is to take early wickets. Once that happens, they panic. And when they panic, only then can we win.' Amarnath nods in agreement.

The peroration is left for the team manager. Man Singh picks up the June issue of *Wisden* and reads out the magazine's preview of the World Cup. The article, written by its editor, David Frith, lists India's record in one-day cricket. They've lost 28 out of the 40 matches they've played so far. The second-worst record amongst all test-playing nations, only behind Sri Lanka. Mr Frith is of the opinion that the International Cricket Conference, or ICC, has done a disservice to cricket by inviting a team as average as India to participate in the premier limited-overs tournament.

There's a sense of unease in the coach. Suddenly, the reclining seats don't feel very comfortable. The naughty gang at the back looks uncharacteristically serious. Kapil is glowering at a large expanse of farmland beside the M1 motorway. Not a word more is spoken. None is needed.

A few miles behind them speeds a Mercedes-Benz, model W123. Unlike the sombre mood in the Indian team bus, the Merc is overflowing with ebullience. Mintu Bhatia, the restaurateur from Southall and the owner of the luxury sedan, sits at the back with a cut glass in hand. Kulwant Singh, his friend, is at the wheel. Mintu rarely allows anyone to drive his car. Not even his son. But tonight, he'd rather sip his Scotch as Kulwant drives. Giving Mintu company is Saran, sipping his whisky, sitting in the passenger seat. In the boot, along with three travel bags, lies an Indian tricolour. The cricket-crazy, India-born British trio is heading to Manchester to watch their team play the Windies. Through India's four practice games, as self-appointed caterers, they enjoyed watching the matches sitting alongside the players. But now that the tournament has started properly, they won't have the luxury of entering the Indian team's dressing room. But spectator stands should be fun too, they are convinced.

Like Jiten Bhai Parekh, Mintu too moved to Britain in the late 1940s, courtesy the British Nationality Act of 1948. As an 18-year-old, semi-literate boy from the hinterland, he began working as a sweeper at the Heathrow airport. Moved up to becoming a waiter at an Indian restaurant. To then owning a restaurant of his own. To now being an owner of two restaurants, a sweet shop and a car dealership in Southall. He is also the president of the Punjabi Association of London. Mintu's success is seen as an inspiration for the growing community of Indians in the UK. Unlike those who came from privileged backgrounds and merged into the English society as lawyers and doctors, the majority of the Indian immigrants belong to the proletariat.

Mintu's rise, in that sense, is also a sign of the rise of the commoner. A minor victory for the stereotyped airport sweeper. He's the pin-up boy for Southall Indians. Except for one. His own son, Harry. Harry has a pin-up of Freddie Mercury in his fancy room – complete with central heating, Bose speakers and a Sony colour TV – in his father's fancy three-storeyed house. Like his hero, Freddie, Harry isn't particularly proud of his Indian heritage. And, like his hero, he's not too keen on his Indian name either. The erstwhile Harjinder Singh Bhatia prefers to go by Harry. Rajma chawal, bhangra and Kapil Dev aren't his things. Give him fish and chips, rock and roll and George Best any day.

It's not been the best week in Jiten Bhai Parekh's 35-year stint in England. After his shop was ransacked and burgled, he's had to make numerous trips to the police station. Even though the crime was witnessed by a handful of people on the street that night, no one has agreed to testify. He's walking back home from another unfruitful trip to the cops, who still haven't nabbed the culprits. His only solace is the 600 pounds in his pocket that he received earlier today from the insurance company. Even that has taken one week of convincing. Insurance companies like to differentiate between shoplifting and theft. The Theft Act of 1968 only covers physical break-ins. Shoplifting, for example, is not included under the shop insurance policy. 'Thank god those rascals pillaged my place that night or else even these 600 pounds...' Jiten Bhai ruminates as he walks towards his house, now just two blocks away. His quick steps come to a halt as a red light flashing from the signboard of a shop in front of him catches his eye.

The betting shop has the odds for the Prudential World Cup displayed outside. The West Indies with the odds of 3:1 are right on top, followed by England, Australia, Pakistan and New Zealand. India is right at the bottom, behind even Sri Lanka, tied with Zimbabwe, at a mouth-watering 66:1.

Jiten Bhai isn't a betting man. His lone source of income – his shop – has been shut for eight days now. He's dipped into his savings to pay for his family's weekly expenditure. The 600 pounds in his pocket will only partially cover the repair costs of the shop. The grim situation he finds himself in has his mind befuddled. He's tired of his exiguous existence. He walks into the bookmakers almost instinctively. He walks out three minutes later. His pockets are empty. A ticket in his hand has 'INDIA: WIN' written on it.

The Indian team is curled up in their beds in the hotel in Manchester. Try as much as he can, Sandeep Patil can't catch a wink. Even two stiff ones of a well-aged Scotch, his usual for the night, isn't helping him calm his nerves. Two weeks before departing for England, playing at the famous Shivaji

Gymkhana, a rising delivery from Pradeep Sundaram had broken his floating rib. The quasi-physios in Indian cricket haven't been of much help since. That he would have to play the World Cup through pain was a reality he had come to accept. Only, playing the West Indian pace battery with an injured rib wasn't something he was prepared for. Gavaskar, his room partner, and someone who has played the Windies pacers with aplomb, is having to answer Patil's barrage of questions on how to tackle Holding, Roberts, Marshall, and Co. 'You've faced Lillee and Thomson before and done well. The West Indians aren't much quicker than them, so don't worry,' are Gavaskar's pearls of wisdom. A measure of spirit is all Patil can offer Gavaskar in return for his contribution in raising his own spirit. But Gavaskar, a connoisseur of wine himself, is staying off ethanol for this tournament. His energies are focussed on his batting. It's the World Cup, after all.

Nerves in control, Patil finally manages to catch some shut eye. Only to have visions of Messrs Holding and Roberts.

9

Well Begun Is Half Done

9 June 1983, Old Trafford, Manchester

It's been an unusually warm summer in England. Today is no different. The sun is out. Yet, Sandeep Patil's mind is clouded with self-doubt.

Balwinder Singh Sandhu is running in and bowling on the match pitch, testing its pace and bounce before the coin toss. 'The pitch seems lively, but the sun beating down may not be so conducive to my style of bowling,' concludes the seam bowler from Bombay.

'How fast are they? Can you see the ball when facing them?' Patil wants to know.

'Look, Sandy, I hooked Marshall for two boundaries in the Jamaica test', says Sandhu confidently. 'If I can do that, you can do it a lot better.'

Patil sees merit in his friend's argument. He is feeling a lot better. 'Bloody! If only I could tell him I actually didn't see the ball while hitting those shots,' Sandhu mutters under his breath.

The West Indian captain, Clive Lloyd, wins the toss and decides to put India in to bat. He wants to play to his strength: unleash the planet's best fast-bowling attack first up.

Ayaz Memon is sitting in the press box. He is rapidly punching away on his typewriter. 'England won toss and decided to bat,' is the first line of his match report. In England to cover the Indian cricket team, he's sitting 200 miles away. At the Oval Cricket Ground. Surrey is his favourite county. Thanks to Jack Hobbs and Ken Barrington – his heroes while growing up. Barrington, in particular, he has fond memories of. Watching him score 149 versus the Combined Universities in Poona remains his favourite childhood cricketing memory. He even ran on to the field to shake hands with his hero after he had picked up two wickets. Because he looked a lot like Jerry Lewis – the American comedian – and made faces just like him, Barrington endeared himself to 10-year-old Ayaz. Today, sitting in the home of Surrey, covering a World Cup game, Ayaz is finding it hard to believe that he is where he is. But that's not the only reason for his excitement. His eyes are sparkling, anticipating the moment when Martin Crowe will step out to bat. Just 21, Crowe has built quite a reputation for himself. His stint with Somerset made for some fine reading for Ayaz, who, as a chronic consumer of cricket, had been bred on a diet of newspapers and writers from Old Blighty.

Kris Srikkanth has given India a rapid start. But, on 14, Michael Holding has him caught behind. Gavaskar and Amarnath now pitch a tent in the middle. Playing old-fashioned cricket. But at 46 for 1, Malcolm Marshall ends the Little Master's 44-ball stay at the crease. In the stands, Mintu Bhatia and friends are on their third pint of the day. Sandeep Patil walks in and guides the ball to fine leg for his first run. No trouble – he can see the ball out of Marshall's hand. Just seeing the ball may not be enough; one-day cricket demands you to score at a brisk pace too. In an effort to push the tempo, Patil is out for 36, clean-bowled by Larry Gomes. But the time he spent at the crease is invaluable. Patil is now rid of his inner demons. India are down to 141 for 5. On a bright, sunny day, good for batting, the part-time slow bowling of Gomes accounts for the Indian skipper's wicket too.

Meanwhile, Ayaz, the lone Indian journalist at the Oval, is busy talking Gandhi. It's been six months since Richard Attenborough's magnum opus released the world over. The movie has been a source of much debate and discussion across England since then. Cricket journalists are no different. 'Was he a saint? How many hours a day did he meditate? Do most people in India still follow Gandhi's 11 vows? Have political leaders in India carried on his traditions? Is Prime Minister Indira Gandhi related to the Mahatma?' These are just some of the queries thrown at Ayaz. The lawyer-turned-journalist isn't much of a Gandhi scholar himself. Yet, he has all the answers. 'Who's gonna corroborate all that I've said anyway?' is what he's telling himself.

One Indian who's surely not following Gandhi's philosophy of non-violence today is Yashpal Sharma. The middle-order batsman is hitting the ball with ferocity, enjoying the pace of the ball coming on to his bat. He's already unleashed a cut, a hook and a pull from his armoury of strokes. The West Indies pace battery doesn't surprise him any more. He's seen plenty of them this summer. The Indian dressing room is cheering every 'badam' shot that this almond-loving batsman is unleashing. Roger Binny is nudging 1s and 2s at the other end. The pair has added 73 crucial runs to the board. 120 balls later, Yashpal is bowled by Holding. But not before despatching 9 balls across the rope. 89 is written beside his name as he walks back to the pavilion. In the last few overs, Madan Lal uses the long-handle bat to good effect. His run-a-ball 21 has pushed India to 262 for 6 in their allotted 60 overs.

The Gandhi fan club congregation at the Oval is interrupted. A member of the press corps has just returned from the BBC radio commentary box at the ground. He's learnt that India have piled a more-than competitive total versus the reigning World Champions. Ayaz promptly gulps whatever remains of the tea in his cup. A radio is organized in the lounge behind the press box. You can't see New Zealand chasing England's 322 from here. But you can hear the West Indies chasing India's 262. Martin Crowe, Ayaz's raison d'être for being at the Oval today, has just walked out to bat. 'Maybe some other time,' Ayaz consoles himself, as he settles down in front of the radio.

There seems to be a role reversal between the West Indian openers today. Desmond Haynes has decided to take the charge of getting quick runs, even as the usually assertive Gordon Greenidge plays for the singles. Suddenly, the sun has disappeared. The more familiar Manchester grey sky now covers the field. The Indian fielders are using generous amounts of saliva to keep the ball's shine intact. The seamers, in anticipation of the ball swinging, are licking their lips.

By the 14th over, the West Indies are 49 for 1. Haynes is run-out. Seven runs later, Greenidge is bowled by Sandhu.

Ayaz finds himself caught in a dichotomy. Excited because India may be on to something here, perturbed because he won't get to witness it. His presupposition that India had no chance in hell of beating the mighty Windies may cost him dearly, he knows.

'Rain stops play!' announces the radio commentator in Manchester. The light starts to deteriorate. An hour later, play is called off for the day. Ayaz breathes a sigh of relief. The West Indies are 67 for 2, from 22 overs. Viv Richards on 12 and Bacchus on 2. Play is rescheduled for tomorrow morning.

Mintu Bhatia and friends, unfortunately, won't be in attendance. They are dog-tired after a day of revelry. Mintu's hands have given up after the non-stop waving of the Indian flag through the day. Plus, each of them has business to attend to. Tomorrow is Friday. Restaurants in Southall get awfully busy over the weekends. Anyway, watching their team more than match up to their more fancied Caribbean counterparts is a win in itself. The actual result – immaterial!

Ayaz is back in the Oval's press box. Martin Crowe is stitching together a masterpiece in front of him. But he's busy writing about Yashpal's masterpiece in Manchester, munching on an English muffin. His office in Bombay has asked him to promptly send the India match report. 'India on Cusp of a Famous Win' will be the *Mid-Day* page-one flyer, the newspaper editor has concluded.

Despite Crowe's magnificent 97, New Zealand have lost by a massive margin of 106 runs. Underlining England's billing as one of the favourites to win the tournament.

Ayaz has just sent his report, making the 1 a.m. deadline back home. Thank god for fax. Oval is one of the three grounds in England to have this new-age technology at its disposal. It allows one to send an image of what one has written to anywhere in the world, real time! Had it been the usual telex – the commonly used device in cricket press boxes around the world – Ayaz's match report wouldn't have made it to the broadsheet the next day.

Wait! India on the verge of upsetting the West Indies isn't the story of the day. World Cup debutants Zimbabwe have beaten the last edition's finalists, Australia, Ayaz is told as he sits down to take a sip of his first drink for the night – a fine blend of malts from the Scottish highlands – a celebration of sorts for keeping his job despite missing the match in Manchester.

'Zimbabwe captain Duncan Fletcher hit 69 off 84 balls as Zimbabwe posted 239/8 in their 60 overs. Australia needed just 4 an over to register a simple win. But Fletcher wasn't done yet. He took 4/42 with his medium pace. Rod Marsh tried his best in the end with a 50 not out, but it wasn't enough. Australia fell short by 13 runs...' the driver of the Indian team coach has just rattled off the entire match report as he drives Kapil and his men back to their hotel in Manchester. An immigrant to the British Isle from Rhodesia, the captain of the bus can't contain his excitement. He followed all the action at Trent Bridge on radio, even as he was parked inside Old Trafford where another World Cup match was being played in front of him. This impromptu news bulletin has the members of the Indian team smiling. Could this be a tournament of upsets?

10 June 1983, Old Trafford

New day, but same ol' Manchester weather: grey skies and cold winds. Not out overnight, Richards and Bacchus walk out to bat. 'We've already got Haynes and Greenidge; all we now need is Viv, and the rest of their batsmen will be susceptible to the moving ball,' is Gavaskar's analysis before everyone in the team spreads out to their fielding positions.

'The West Indies need 196 off 228,' reads the score sheet. Ayaz picks up his copy in the press box. He took the early morning train from London to Manchester, and now sits on his designated seat before the first ball of the day is bowled, still grateful to the almighty that his indiscretion yesterday – of going to the Oval instead of Old Trafford – hasn't cost him his job.

The day's play starts with Vivian Richards on 12 and Faoud Bacchus on 2. Before Ayaz can finish his first cup of English breakfast tea, the West Indies are 124 for 6. All five top-order batsmen got a start, reached double figures, but failed to go past 25. Thankfully for them, skipper Clive Lloyd is still at the crease. Or is he? Roger Binny has just slipped one past the left-hander's defence and shattered his stumps. 130 for 8 now. On an overcast day, the Indian seamers are making merry. 27 runs later, the stumps have been disturbed once again. This time it's Ravi Shastri's doing, who's sent Michael Holding back into the hut. The West Indies still need 106 runs more with only the last pair standing at the crease. The Indian team driver starts to warm up the bus engine; most of the fans who returned for the second day of the match are beginning to leave the stadium. Ayaz is winding up his work. Only that an hour and a half later, the bus is still at the stadium, a handful of fans are still watching a match and Ayaz is still typing away at his desk.

Pace twins, Andy Roberts and Joel Garner, are pacing their innings too. Roberts, with his trademark batting stance of putting his entire body weight on the shoulder of his bat, is shouldering the burden by taking singles. Garner, at the other end, is using the long-handle to good effect. He has a 6 to show for his efforts. They are now 35 runs short with 36 balls to go. Garner now steps out of the crease to face Shastri. The Big Bird plans to send another one flying over the ropes. But he's beaten by the flight. Before the 6-foot–8-inch batsman can drag his feet back into the crease, wicketkeeper Kirmani has the bails off in a flash. Garner is out for 37. Roberts is left stranded on 37. The 71-run stand by the last wicket is a new World Cup record.

For India, this is only their second win in a World Cup in seven attempts. The first, in 1975, against a bunch of amateurs from a collection of four East African nations, wasn't much to write home about. This is the real thing!

Yet, the Indian team is subdued as it heads to its dressing room, situated on the right wing of the main pavilion made of red bricks. Mindful of the fact that they've had a narrow escape, despite being in a commanding position at the start of the day.

'Yashpal's knock took the game away from us. The fact that he got runs in a long tour of the Windies helped him get used to our bowlers,' is how Viv Richards sums up the match on BBC Radio's live coverage, visibly smarting from his team's first-ever loss in a World Cup.

Jiten Bhai turns off the radio in his London apartment. Gets up from his living room couch and rushes towards the bathroom. His faded blue shirt hangs on a hook on the bathroom door. He puts his hand into the front pocket and pulls out the betting slip he had purchased two days ago. It's crumpled, but not torn. He flattens the piece of paper between his palms, straightening it. He then walks over to the wooden wardrobe in the bedroom. Unlocks the small drawer hidden at the back, behind a pile of shirts. Places the slip alongside a gold-plated vintage watch, a diamond-studded ring and a miniature idol of Lord Krishna made of silver. He locks the drawer before putting the keys back in his wallet.

At Old Trafford, Kris Srikkanth is in the shower when it hits him! He lets out a scream, 'Come on, guys! Do you realize we've beaten the World Champions!' With the adrenaline from the match wearing down, it is beginning to sink in for every member of the side. 'We've beaten the champions, we've beaten the champions' – the walls of the Old Trafford dressing room echoes the tune of the English band Queen's famous hit from five years ago.

Long after the singing and the dancing, captain Kapil is sitting in the dressing room, alone, soaking in the feeling of having masterminded one of the biggest upsets in World Cup history. Only now is he convinced that the win in Berbice, two months ago, wasn't a fluke. He can already envision a World Cup semi-final featuring India. Sitting just 500 metres away from the current FA Cup champions, Manchester United's 'Theatre of Dreams', Kapil, a keen footballer himself, is allowing himself the luxury of dreaming just that little bit.

The British media though is ensuring that Kapil and Co. don't end up hallucinating. The headline of the *Times* the following day reads: 'The Favourites Pay Heavily for Their Complacency', suggesting that the West Indies's loss at Manchester was down to their own failings rather than India's brilliance. The British press, on the whole, has dubbed the 34-run win as a 'flash in the pan'.

10

Speed Breaker

11 June 1983, Grace Road, Leicester

The Indian dressing room is as buoyant as it was exactly 24 hours ago. Their tournament score reads: Two matches, two wins. The match at Leicester today, against Zimbabwe, was billed as the 'battle of the giant-killers'. Like India, who beat the mighty Windies, Zimbabwe beat Australia on the opening day of the tournament. Today though, they did not have it in them – India wrapped up the game in just the 38th over, chasing down Zimbabwe's 155, with five wickets to spare.

Kapil Dev was lucky to begin with, winning the toss and putting the Africans in to bat on a miserable, overcast day. Now he stands in the centre of the Indian dressing room, addressing his team after a dominating performance. He begins by acknowledging the role of seamers Madan Lal and Roger Binny, who polished off half the Zimbabwean side. Madan, in fact, is the Man of the Match for his figures of 3/27.

'Good job, Madan and Roger. Pitch wet, ball wet, you still get swing from ball, and bounce in right areas,' Kapil starts off.

'Because of rain, match stopped again and again. Keeping batsman concentration not easy in these times, but, Sandy, you still bat long. Good job!' Kapil congratulates Sandeep Patil for his half-century, the highest score by a batsman from either side today.

All this while, Kirti Azad is standing behind Kapil, out of his line of sight, enacting a catch in the slips after every grammatically incorrect line his skipper utters – a visual metaphor for 'slip of tongue', so to say. The rest of the team is trying its best to stifle its laughter, but without much success.

Undeterred, Kapil carries on. 'Let's also clap for new record holder, Kirmani; someone tell me he is the first man to take five catches in a World Cup game.' Applause and whistles follow.

Gavaskar is clapping, but not quite following. Staring out of the dressing room window. Musing.

Earlier in the day, the Little Master fell to the raw pace of Peter Rawson for 4, caught at slip, off the glove. This has come after his not-so-fluent 19 versus the West Indies in the first match. Rawson looked threatening today, dismissing the other opener, Kris Srikkanth, also early. Unfortunately, he had to leave the field soon after his fine opening spell with a strain, leaving the Zimbabweans wondering what might have been had he been allowed to bowl his full quota of 12 overs.

'Come on, boys, the bus is ready,' manager Man Singh cuts short the revelry.

A large crowd of expat Indians is gathered outside the dressing room to catch a glimpse of their heroes as they board the bus. Mintu Singh Bhatia from Southall is amongst them. It almost felt like a home game for India, owing to the large Indian community in Leicester. Even the poor weather couldn't discourage them from attending today's game. And their constant vocal support for their team was, at times, almost intimidating for the Zimbabweans.

Syed Kirmani and Roger Binny are busy signing autographs. The women in the crowd are swooning over Mohinder 'Jimmy' Amarnath and Sandeep Patil. Amarnath is uncomfortable, almost hiding behind his raised collar. Patil is enjoying the attention, flashing a flirtatious half-smile. Mintu Bhatia has caught hold of Madan Lal and Yashpal Sharma, and has convinced them to visit Southall once they are back in London. Kapil is waving to the crowd as he walks towards the bus.

Metres away, Zimbabwean players Andy Pycroft and Robin Brown are having to explain to the media why Zimbabwe lost. Pycroft, who scored 14 today, thinks the top order threw their wickets away, trying to hit the ball over the top. Wicketkeeper–batsman Brown, who scored 6, is of the opinion that they were looking for too many boundaries, rather than concentrating on working the 1s and 2s.

Gavaskar is the last one out of the dressing room. Spotting him, Ali Shah, the Zimbabwean opener, makes a dash for it. He's been an admirer of the Little Master for years. Good time for a small chat, he reckons. Shah's 'hello' is met by a blank look as Gavaskar walks past his opposite number and straight into the front row of the team bus. As Shah watches his idol stare out of the bus window, brooding, he suspects the snub may have been inadvertent.

The bus is starting to fill up. Srikkanth is the last to enter. And just as he'd fallen to the pace and swing of Rawson a few hours ago, he's fallen on the floor of the bus, failing to negotiate the last step. The entire team is in splits. Not Gavaskar. Srikkanth is helped on to his feet by the driver. His kitbag lay on top of him, making it difficult for him to get up on his own. This isn't the first time the opener has lost his balance, and everyone who's laughing their lungs out suspect that this may not be the last either.

Binny, the designated keeper of the little fridge inside the coach, has stocked it sufficiently with pints of lager. Srikkanth is rendering his own version of 'Mere jeevan saathi' – the hit Hindi song from the famous Bollywood film Ek Duuje Ke Liye – complete with the Tamil accent, just as director K. Balachander had meant it to be. His teammates are cheering him on. Some humming along. Carefree. The luxury coach is on its way.

Kirti has slid in an unmarked VHS tape into the shiny, new Sony VCR installed in the front of the bus, goaded on by the members of the naughty gang – Patil and Sandhu, sitting right at the back.

The X-rated images that have appeared on the screen seem to have taken the seniors in the front by surprise… At first. But a second look at the obstreperous environment around, and the skipper reckons bawdy may just be the right kind of entertainment for a night like tonight.

Gavaskar is still absent. Looking at the English countryside go by.

Ten miles into their journey, minutes after they've pushed back their backrests and snuggled into their sofa-like chairs, beers in hand, the driver slams the breaks. 'What happened?' the team manager wants to know. 'Cops, boss,' says the driver. 'Maybe they've noticed I am not wearing my seat belt.' The UK made seat belts mandatory for the driver and the front-seat passenger just a couple of months ago. The populace is still to get used to it.

The highway patrol that overtook them seconds ago is now parked in front of the bus. The sun is setting. The sky is a shade of dark blue. The blue film has been turned off. Two men in dark blue tunics with polished silver buttons, and matching dark blue trousers with a sewn-in pocket for the baton, enter the bus. 'What have you guys got playing on the screen?' asks the taller one. 'Worse still, you haven't even drawn your curtains,' says the other. 'We've received three complaints already from people travelling on this route.'

The sun has set. The sky is bright red. As are a few faces in the official World Cup team bus. Manager Man Singh has been called in for the rescue again. The bus has begun to lay rubber over the asphalt again. Much beer is being guzzled again. The video player is playing again. This time, it's Amitabh Bachchan crooning '*Jahan teri yeh nazar hai, meri jaan mujhe khabar hai*'.

11

Huge Defeat to Hughes & Co.

13 June 1983, Trent Bridge, Nottingham

It's a cold day in Nottingham. Sunil Gavaskar gets up from his seat in the dressing room, walks towards his kitbag and bends down to pull out his batting gloves. It's a bit of a stretch. The coffin lies beside another player's kit, making it inaccessible for his relatively small arms. Summoning the gymnast in him, his outstretched right arm finally grabs hold of the gloves. Synchronously, the 5-foot–5-inch Gavaskar can feel his hamstring stiffen. He sits down instantly. Allowing the muscle to relax.

'It's just a muscle pull; I can bat, but am not sure about running and fielding. I'd rather not be a liability on the field,' Gavaskar is quick to inform the management. Dilip Vengsarkar is drafted into the playing XI.

The field is covered in mist. The moisture from the river Trent, which flows alongside the ground, being the prime contributor. There's still an hour to go before the coin toss. The Indian team, without Gavaskar, heads out to warm up. Mohinder Amarnath is leading the pack, demonstrating a set of stretching exercises, which the rest are following to a T. The trials and tribulations of managing an inelastic body over the years have taught Amarnath various techniques that allow him to compete at the highest levels, despite the constant stiffness in his body. His mates are making the most of his acquired expertise. This is an unusual sight ahead of an India match. Knocking – the art of driving balls gingerly thrown at you – is more the Indian way of getting ready for a match; more so, if you are a player from the country's most-productive cricket nursery, Bombay. In that sense, this tournament is a new beginning for the Indian team as far as the approach towards fitness is concerned. Those associated with Indian cricket suggest it's the legacy of Hemu Adhikari, the former test cricketer-turned-coach, who instilled the need for prematch fitness routines in all the Under-19 camps held across the country, through which some of the current national team players have also graduated.

The Australians are stretching their limbs on the opposite side of the ground. Without Dennis Lillee. The star fast bowler has arrived late to the ground and is getting into his whites. He doesn't need to, he's informed. He's been dropped for this game.

Lillee hasn't been travelling in the bus along with the rest of the team. He chooses his own transport. According to one Australian journalist, 'Lillee feels he is bigger than the team.' He doesn't get along very well with Kim Hughes either. His dislike towards his skipper was evident during the Australian team's net session a few months ago, when he bombarded Hughes with a series of bouncers even as he bowled run-of-the-mill stuff to every other batsman. One such bouncer caught Hughes on the arm. Lillee walked up to him and said, 'Sorry.' Hughes kept his cool and replied, 'Oh, that's fine.' Only for Lillee to snarl back, 'Sorry I didn't fuckin' hit ya!'

Lillee's biggest grouse is that Hughes is captain ahead of his best mate, and the team's vice captain, Rod Marsh. In fact, there is palpable dissonance within the Aussie camp. The entire team is split down the middle; divided on the basis of those who played and those who skipped Kerry Packer's World Series Cricket. Kim Hughes is the undeclared golden boy of the Australian Cricket Board, or the ACB. Lillee, Marsh, Jeff Thomson and other such seniors, who chose a big pay cheque over playing cricket for the ACB, may have been inducted back into the national side, but are having to pay the price for their supposed treason by playing under a captain many years their junior.

Infighting isn't the only thing plaguing the Aussies. They've come to the World Cup with almost zero preparation. They had no training camp before their departure to England. The Australian winter wasn't conducive for the players to practise on their own either. The national team's lone three-day practice match, versus New Zealand, was abandoned because of a hailstorm.

But the biggest storm Hughes and his team have had to face came about just yesterday. An event from which they are yet to recover. A 101-run loss to the West Indies. A retribution of sorts after the reigning World Champions' unexpected loss to India in their opening match. The loss aside, the manner in which the Kangaroos were brought to their knees by the Caribbean pacers hasn't done much to the confidence of a team that is already battling internal turmoil. Holding used his lethal bouncer to send opener Graeme Wood to the hospital with a concussion. And Winston Davis, playing only his second ODI, and whom the Indians had handled with ease at Berbice, broke the backbone of the Australian batting order, finishing with 7/51 – the best figure for any bowler in World Cup history. 'Winston Davis, the West Indies's latest fast-bowling discovery sent a shiver of fear through every team in the Prudential World Cup,' is how the *Daily Express* puts it.

Tomorrow's headline is about to be written.

Ayaz is handed the team sheet in the Trent Bridge press box. There is no Gavaskar in the playing XI. He reads the paper again. Seconds later, his hands are busy punching away on his typewriter. He has his lead story even before a single ball is bowled.

Once bitten twice shy, Ayaz, after committing the blunder of missing India's first match, has been diligently attending all of India's games, and plans to not break the routine for the rest of the tournament. Even though travelling to venues outside London involves buying expensive tickets for the British rail, which is threatening to upset Ayaz's meagre budget. But, for the moment, he's found a solution. Moving into Imtiaz Ansari's house in Surbiton – a few train stops away from Wimbledon – has allowed Ayaz to save up on his daily rent at the YMCA hostel. Imtiaz is a young engineer, and a friend of Ayaz's from Bombay. He's currently in London on a work permit. Making just enough money to sustain a bachelor's life. And considering the fairly small distances in England, Ayaz can afford to travel back to London, each night, from wherever he is covering the game. That apart, he's enjoying Imtiaz's company; Imtiaz is a sport nut himself – cricket, tennis, football, his host can talk endlessly about the latest trends in his favourite sports. 'For a sports buff, there is no place like England,' he's told Ayaz a few times in the last couple of days. His guest can't help but feel envious.

On the field, Kim Hughes finds himself in the unenvious position of having lost two out of the two games his team has played so far. Today though, he's started with a win – the toss. Australia are batting. Not surprising, considering the team lost to minnows Zimbabwe on the same ground just four days ago after deciding to bat second.

It's Monday morning, England aren't playing. Only a thin crowd is in attendance at Trent Bridge. There are more sports fans across the road from the cricket stadium. At the City Ground, home to Nottingham Forest Football Club. They've finished fifth in the Premier League that ended just a month ago. Manager Brian Clough and his team are busy signing autographs. The fans are grateful to their team for having qualified for the UEFA Cup, the second tier in Europe's top-flight football. Especially because they lost one of their biggest stars, Peter Shilton, to Southampton in a record deal worth £325,000 at the beginning of the season. It's a regular meet-and-greet session. A typical off-season, fan-building exercise.

Kepler Wessels can't exercise restraint. He tries to cut a Kapil Dev outswinger only to inside edge the ball on to his stumps. Australia are 11 for 1. Kapil has set an aggressive field. Two slips, and only two fielders are outside the 30-yard circle: third man and fine leg. These are the new rules that the Indian captain has to adjust to. It is, after all, the first one-day tournament to feature a fielding circle: an oval, 30 yards away from the stumps.

Seeing the boundary rope unmanned, Trevor Chappell hits a cracker of a drive between cover and extra cover for 4. It elicits a 'good shot' from Richie Benaud in the commentary box. The drive is followed by a pull off Ravi Shastri's short-pitched left-arm spin that hits the boundary rope, splitting the square-leg and midwicket fielders perfectly. Shastri's first 2 overs have leaked 16 runs. Barring a couple of run-out opportunities, Hughes and Chappell haven't given even a sniff of a wicket to the Indian bowlers. Trevor, the youngest of the three famous Chappell brothers, is wearing his baggy green and has chosen a more carefree approach. Hughes wears a helmet, remains circumspect, and is cleverly sneaking in the 1s and 2s.

Ayaz, in the meantime, has sneaked into the Indian dressing room, chasing the bigger story of the day – why isn't Gavaskar playing? One look at him – sitting in one corner of the changing room, watching the on-field proceedings frigidly – and Ayaz knows he better not broach the subject with the man. Ayaz, like most others who are in any way involved with Indian cricket, is familiar with Gavaskar's mercurial moods. His two best mates from Bombay, Dilip Vengsarkar and Sandeep Patil, are on the field at the moment, and can't possibly help him with any hints about what might have transpired inside the team, which has led to Gavaskar not playing. He tries his luck with Man Singh instead, slipping in the Gavaskar question while making casual conversation. But the former cricketer-turned-manager blocks his query with a bat as straight as Gavaskar's, and offers only a sly smile in return.

Hughes, all this while blocking and running, has changed gears. He charges down the pitch to Madan Lal and smashes one towards the cover boundary. The ball speeds along the ground and collides with the boundary rope. The velocity sending it 10 feet up in the air, over the heads of three overenthusiastic spectators, who have run in from the stands to try and get a feel of the match ball.

The next delivery, the ball, bruised from the shot before, swings in, breaching Hughes's watertight defence and crashes into the stumps with the same speed as the shot before. Madan Lal, the victor of this mini battle, stands in the middle of the pitch with his chest puffed out. Hughes is walking back, head down.

Chappell has his head tilting upwards as he hooks a Mohinder Amarnath short ball to fine leg for an easy single. He now looks further skywards while experiencing something he's never felt before: the joy of completing an international century, his first ever. He's eventually out for 110 off a Mohinder Amarnath outswinger, caught at point by Kris Srikkanth. He's done well to grab hold of a booming cut shot that was dropping on him. He stays on his knees a wee bit longer than usual, trying to figure out how that ball got stuck in his hands.

The giant, black, manually operated scoreboard, with a new-age tall corporate building in the background, reads 260 in 50 overs. With the last 10 overs coming up, and five wickets in hand, Kapil expects an Australian onslaught. The field is spread with all but four fielders manning the boundary rope. The new rules require at least four fielders to be inside the 30-yard circle at all times.

Graham Yallop has a plan. He dances down the pitch to dispatch Balwinder Singh Sandhu past the midwicket boundary, his trademark white helmet intact. The man, known to be the first to wear a helmet in international cricket, after suffering a broken jaw off a Colin Croft bouncer, has the green *patka*-wearing Sandhu seeing red. Nottingham, famous for Robin Hood's swordsmanship, is now witnessing Yallop's batsmanship. Australia cross the magical 300-run mark.

Against the flow of runs, the Indian skipper finishes well; picking up two tailenders in the penultimate over of the Australian innings to end with the figures of 5/43. But the Kangaroos finish stronger. Yallop hits two boundaries on either side of the wicket to remain 66*. Playing his 21st ODI, it is the 31-year-old's highest ODI score. Australia have notched up 320 for 9 in their 60 overs. Yallop walks off to a standing ovation. The crowd is gradually building up.

The decibel levels matching those that the adjoining football stadium witnessed a couple of hours back. All in anticipation of a big run chase by an Indian team filled with all-rounders.

Ayaz has returned to his press box chair. After his unsuccessful attempts at extracting information out of the Indian dressing room, he made a detour to Larwood & Voce, a pub tucked away in a corner of the stadium, named after the two protagonists of the infamous 1932–33 Bodyline Series, famed for its beef roast. One bite into the well-done T-bone and Ayaz knows he made the right decision. Of skipping the regular fare at the press box in favour of a local delicacy. Now, he's ready to witness the Indian batting. Who's opening instead of Gavaskar is the first thing he is keen to know.

Out walks the all-rounder in the making, Ravi Shastri, along with Kris Srikkanth. 38 runs later, he's out for 11. Caught on the crease, with no footwork, to an inswinging delivery; struck on his pads, plumb in front. Symptomatic of a makeshift opener. Someone who batted number 10 in India's opening match of the tournament.

38 for 1 quickly becomes 43 for 2. Mohinder Amarnath is run-out. Kris Srikkanth, at the striker's end, begins to run after hitting the ball to point, only to change his mind seconds later. Too late. Jimmy is already standing next to him.

Vengsarkar's tournament debut isn't going to plan. He plants his left leg across the middle stump to flick Ken MacLeay, but misses the line of the ball. He's nervously waiting for the umpire's decision. The bowler knows he's got his man. The umpire answers in the affirmative. India is now 57 for 3. And before another run can be added to the board, Sandeep Patil is bowled through the wide gap between his bat – sporting the Symonds sticker – and pad. MacLeay bags one more.

Srikkanth is batting on 39 after facing 62 balls. He needs to push the tempo. Down on one knee, he tries to send the ball out of the ground, sweeping against the left-arm spin of Tom Hogan. Only, the ball hits the top edge of his bat and lands safely in the hands of Allan Border at mid-on. His is the first wicket in the match to fall to a spinner, on a day that India's lone spinner, Ravi Shastri, on the back of some ordinary bowling, was allowed only 2 overs by his skipper.

Hogan and his spin aren't done yet. Kapil has kept the entertainment going, smashing 40 from just 26 balls. Like Srikkanth, he too attempts a sweep. But the ball escapes his bat, ricochets off his body, hits the back of his bat and lands on the stumps. India are 124 for 7, after Yashpal Sharma was out a few overs ago, caught and bowled by MacLeay.

That MacLeay has picked up Syed Kirmani, the last Indian wicket to fall on the day, only seems fair. In the absence of pace twins Lillee and Thompson, the medium-pacer has bowled an immaculate line and length, finishing the day with 6/39; India are 158 all out. Marginally more than what

Trevor Chappell alone managed to score on the day. His 110 has ensured he is the Man of the Match. It's the first time in two years that this Chappell is making the headlines. The last time was when he bowled an underarm ball – on the insistence of his brother and captain, Greg Chappell – to deny New Zealand's Brian McKechnie a 6 off the last ball of a match. Two years later, it remains one of the ugliest incidents witnessed on the cricket field.

In Robin Hood country, Kapil Dev and his merrymen have tasted their first defeat of the tournament. It's not an upset in any way. Not for the players, the fans or the press.

Knowing the match has played out to form, Ayaz wants to devote more time to writing the Gavaskar story than to the usual match report. He understands the demands of a cricket fan in India, or so he thinks. But he surely isn't understanding what's happening inside the Indian dressing room: Why did Gavaskar not play this game? Was he dropped? Is there friction between him and Kapil?

'No, he was rested,' was the only sentence the press managed to extract out of Man Singh, before he climbed on to the team bus and left for London, a short while ago.

To write a 600-word front-page story, a mere one-line quote won't suffice. So, Ayaz jots down all that he knows, suspects and understands of the Gavaskar story so far, in bullet points:

- Kapil and Gavaskar have a hot-and-cold relationship, that's for sure.
- Gavaskar hasn't had the best of times with the bat in this tournament.
- One can gauge he is under pressure to perform. Whether that pressure is external or self-imposed, who knows?
- Sometimes, if Gavaskar is scowling, it is not because Kapil is captain, but because he isn't doing well... Maybe?
- It could very well be Gavaskar's self-obsession to score runs. The man is a perfectionist, after all.
- Gavaskar is an intense person anyway. He can be a brooder, he can be a loner, he can isolate himself.

After going through what he's just typed one final time, Ayaz rubs his hands. There's enough meat for a juicy story. But only a couple of hours to type and telex it to his office in Bombay, before catching the last train to London, where India play their next match, against the wounded West Indies.

There are no wounds for the Indian team to nurse. A loss against the Australians was neither hurtful nor shocking. The bunch is headed to Coventry, an hour's journey from their hotel in Nottingham. Kapil's friend Ravi Sanghera is their host for the evening. Ravi is an off-spinner himself, and plays for minor counties as a professional. There is home-made Punjabi food for dinner. Syed Kirmani is looking dapper in a black suit, wearing a wig and smoking a pipe, sitting next to the swimming pool. As are the rest of the players, enjoying their choice of beverage. Sandhu has his eyes on Kapil sipping from his glass, his arm flexing with each sip. He finally musters enough courage to ask his skipper what has him puzzled. 'How is it that your skin is thinner than mine in the biceps area?' A couple of seconds is all Kapil needs for a retort: 'That is because I am not as thick-skinned as you, sardar.' A swell of laughter follows, just as a riposte of that quality deserves. Only, the plaudits aren't coming Kapil's way.

Everyone is looking in the direction of the pool. Syed Kirmani stands in the centre, neck-deep in water, pipe extinguished, wig floating. Who pushed him in? No one saw. Roger Binny is next. Pushed in by Kirti Azad. This, everyone saw. Ravi Shastri comes rushing from the bar. 'What happened?' he asks. 'This,' says Kirti, and demonstrates. The rest of the team enjoys a belly laugh. At Kirti, expletives are hurled. Binny and Shastri scamper out of the pool. Kirti runs for cover. Kirmani Bhai – floating mane aside – remains unflustered. He has taken off his tie, thrown his pipe aside, removed his shoes and is doing laps of the pool.

12

Gen X versus Gen Ex

14 June 1983, London

Jiten Bhai is sitting at the cash counter. Back after a forced hiatus of two weeks. That's how long it's taken to fix his ransacked shop. Despondency from what happened on that fateful day of 1 June apart, he finds himself in a lugubrious mood today. His 16-year-old daughter, Pooja, who's accompanied him to the store, is the cause for this melancholy. The devoted father would rather have her spend her school holidays pursuing her passion – music – than help around at the shop.

Pooja is a talented pianist. The soul of her school choir. She's just cleared her higher secondary exams and aims to join the prestigious Royal Academy of Music to pursue their highly acclaimed undergraduate programme. All she's ever dreamt of is to be a part of the institute that produced her idol, Elton John, amongst a host of other world-renowned musicians. It won't be easy, Pooja knows. There's a stringent procedure in place, which ensures that only the best make the cut. But she has faith in her craft. All she needs is a couple of months of private lessons and she's confident of cracking 'The Academy's' code.

Private piano lessons in London cost 15 pounds an hour. 150 pounds a week. Unaffordable for the petty bourgeois club of London, of which Jiten Bhai Parekh is a chief patron. More so now, after the shop was burgled. And the 600-pound compensation from the insurance company? That could help. Oh, but that's turned into a piece of paper! A lottery ticket. Issued by the largest chain of bookmakers in the United Kingdom. A decision Jiten Bhai is beginning to regret every time he sees his daughter use her gifted hands to lift a bottle of vino, a tin of tobacco or a shampoo, instead of working a crescendo, allegro or legato.

Pooja herself seems in high spirits, arranging the newly arrived stock on the shelves, humming Duran Duran's biggest single of the year, 'Rio'. If not at the piano lessons, she would much rather be at her father's side. Her mom, Sarla Parekh, has also insisted. 'What if another untoward incident happens?' is her fear. Highly probable in the current scenario. Paki-bashing is in vogue. Having a co-worker could prove to be the difference between a mere assault and a fatality. Once bitten, the Parekh family isn't taking any chances.

The British media isn't helping the situation; rather, it is fuelling the anti-immigrant rhetoric. While state authorities are culpable of under-reporting racist attacks. And the police are prone to harassing the victims, and are even guilty of being involved in the violence at times.

Andha Kanoon, reads the poster on top of Liberty Cinema in the west London suburb of Southall, 12 miles from Jiten Bhai's shop at Baker Street. Bollywood megastar Amitabh Bachchan, dressed in a white shirt, holding a sword dripping with blood, and Hema Malini, the heart-throb of millions, wearing a police officer's uniform, are in the centre of the film's poster. Along with them stands a man wearing a black leather jacket. A debutant from the south Indian film industry. 'Some fellow called Rajinikanth,' the locals say.

There are no film shows at Liberty today. In fact, there hasn't been one for months. The poster outside is of the last film to have been screened at this 70-year-old cinema. No one has bothered pulling it down. In the '60s and '70s, Liberty and Dominion – another cinema in Southall – were the only two theatres in all of London that screened Indian films; each attracting 8000 cinemagoers a week and playing host to some of the biggest stars from Bollywood. But the

'80s saw the emergence of the home video, resulting in fewer and fewer people venturing out to watch a film. With it sounded the death knell for cinemas across London. Liberty, Dominion included.

Today, Liberty functions as a makeshift indoor market. On days, it also doubles up as a community centre for the local Indian populace. This afternoon is one such occasion. Two Indian stars are in the house. Not the Bollywood variety, but cricket stars. Madan Lal and Yashpal Sharma. Important enough to have Southall Indians turn up in large numbers on a working Tuesday afternoon. The felicitation ceremony, organized by the Punjabi Association of London, of which Mintu Bhatia is the president, is honouring two fellow Punjabis for their services to Indian cricket – the team of choice for thousands of British Indians living in Southall. And for the British Indians who live elsewhere in the UK.

Southall is the biggest hub of Indians living in the UK. Dubbed 'Chhota Punjab', it houses the largest Punjabi community outside Asia. Almost 70 per cent of Southall's total population of 70,000 belongs to this gregarious and enterprising community. It all started with a single shop owner, Pritam Singh Sangha. He opened for business in 1954, the only Indian shop in London at the time. It sowed the seeds of a revolution that would see the Asian corner shop become an integral part of the British topography.

By 1960, there were approximately 1,000 Punjabis living in Southall. Nearly all men. Most of whom worked at the R Woolf Rubber Company in neighbouring Hayes. The company's general manager had served with Sikh soldiers during the Second World War, and was a fan of their commitment and diligence.

There is plenty of talk about the Punjabi spirit at Liberty today. Madan and Yashpal's vernacular oration has helped boost the esprit de corps in the hall. Especially in today's times, when skinhead terror has engulfed the country. Frequent attacks by violent gangs opposing immigration, or 'Paki-bashing' as it's being called, have led to a state of despondency amongst the South Asians. The formation of a far-right, fascist political party called the British Nationalist Party, or BNP, in the recent years, has only made matters worse. One such attack happened a few metres away from where today's function is taking place.

Hamburg Tavern, a local pub on the main street of Southall, dubious for its reputation for refusing entry to non-whites, was the venue of one of the ugliest race riots in recent times. Two years ago, more than 200 skinheads travelled to Southall by bus from east London for a 'white power' concert. A few of them smashed shop windows and shouted neo-Nazi slogans, while using bricks and clubs to attack the Asian youths who had gathered in opposition to the gig. The Southall locals threw petrol bombs and other objects in retaliation. Five hours of rioting left 120 people injured and the tavern burnt down.

The 500 British Indians at Liberty are giving a standing ovation to their cricketing heroes as they begin climbing down from the stage. After the speeches, garlands and songs, it's time for high tea. A British custom; but here, the Earl Grey, scones and finger sandwiches are missing. The Indian avatar on offer this afternoon features masala chai with milk and sugar premixed, along with generous helpings of samosas, jalebis and pakoras as accompaniments. All courtesy Mintu Bhatia's Sher-e-Punjab, the most popular restaurant on the broadway. The official photographer on duty is overworked, asked to click pictures every second. Husbands are introducing overenthusiastic wives. Children are jostling for autographs. Teenagers are seeking cricket tips. And Madan and Yashpal are obliging everyone, in between sips of steaming chai. The hall is buzzing.

A loud shattering of glass brings the hubbub to an abrupt halt. It's followed by a lady's scream. A large stone, wrapped in paper, has landed near the foot of the terrified middle-aged woman; brushing past her Patiala salwar and missing her *jutti* – embroidered with real gold and silver threads – by a whisker. No one is hurt. The foreign object made its journey from the main street outside – breaking through the central glass of a large panel, comprising three giant-sized frames, on the road-facing wall of Liberty Cinema, known for its distinct Chinese architecture.

There's commotion in the hall. The saree-clad MC asks the audience not to panic. They oblige. Mintu Bhatia and four others from the organizing committee run out to the main street. Mintu spots a red convertible with four youths inside, heading down the broadway having just gone past Liberty. The two punks at the back are flipping him the bird. A fellow organizer hands him the paper-wrapped stone. 'Piss off, you Pakis,' reads the crushed piece of paper.

The festivities are cut short. The safety of the guests is of primary importance. Madan and Yashpal have been escorted to their cars. Not before long, they are on their way to their hotel in central London. The incident has left a bitter taste in the mouths of everyone involved – the jalebis that were served notwithstanding. More so inside Mintu. His soul hurts. He has recognized the car carrying the mischief-makers. It was a third-generation Pontiac Firebird. He recognizes it all too well. He is the owner!

Harry, aka Harjinder Singh Bhatia, is at the wheel, cruising past the stores and restaurants on the broadway, including his father's Sher-e-Punjab; 'We will rock you', Queen's latest, is blaring from the two-door convertible's woofers. His three English friends complete the quartet that just threw the stone at the Indian gathering. They are Harry's childhood buddies. True-blue English lads. Like Harry himself. Harry's parents might be Indian, but he's not. Born and raised in England, he's only brown on the outside; inside, he's all white. He despises his parents romanticizing the land of their birth, trying to force their Indian culture down his throat. 'What's there to like about India?' he would argue while growing up. Filthy streets, bullock carts on the road, abject poverty all round – that's what India meant to him. He hated his annual trips to their ancestral village in Punjab. He was embarrassed to speak about them to his friends in primary school. Instead, he would make up stories about going to USA, Italy or France on vacation. Soon, that would stop too. As he grew older, he would refuse to travel to India with his parents. Heading to other parts of Europe with his friends became the norm. Of course, all paid for by his Indian father.

'What were you doing outside Liberty Cinema today?' a fuming Mintu wants to know as soon as he sits down for dinner at home.

'Nothing,' replies Harry with a shrug.

'I saw you.'

'Saw me doing what?'

'Didn't you and your nincompoop friends throw that stone inside the building?'

Harry puts down his spoonful of minced pork.

'You saw that?'

'I was inside the theatre, you bloody fool!'

'What! Doing what?'

'That's not the answer to my question, Harjinder.'

'How was I supposed to know you were in there, Dad? We thought it was one of those preachy sermons about the Indian value system. The kind of shit me and my mates hate. This is England, for god's sake! Why can't these people go back to that shithole called India if they want to live a certain way. If you are in England, then conform to the ways of the society. Period!'

'Harji, don't speak to your father like that,' intervenes Pamma Bhatia.

'But, Mom, it's true…'

'Enough, Harjinder,' Mintu interjects. 'You've embarrassed me to no end today. Thank god no one else knows you were part of that rogue bunch. Or else, I'd never be able to face my own people ever again.'

'Oh come on, Dad, stop being melodramatic. It was just a taunt.'

'A taunt? Do you know who was in that hall today? Madan Lal and Yashpal Sharma.'

'Madan and Yashpal, who?'

'Pamma, what a dolt you have for a son.'

'Harji, they are members of the Indian cricket team, beta, playing the World Cup.'

'Cricket World Cup?' sniggers Harry, wearing a Manchester United T-shirt. 'As if I care.'

13

Back to Reality

15 June 1983, London

Croydon is to the Caribbeans what Southall is to the Indians. The southernmost borough of England is home to a large number of Caribbean immigrants. Immigrants who first arrived aboard the SS *Empire Windrush* on 22 June 1948, in Essex. The 8000-mile journey saw 492 passengers from Jamaica, Trinidad and Tobago, and other islands make the trip to the UK, invited by the English after labour shortages post-World War II plagued the island nation. They later came to be known as the 'Windrush Generation'. That generation, of mostly ex-servicemen, found work in manufacturing, construction and public transport, and the women worked as nurses. Thirty-five years and an additional 6,00,000 immigrants later, these still remain the jobs that keep the Afro-Caribbeans in the UK engaged.

And cricket has them engaged today. Not all, but a large majority; if not at the ground, they can be found then in front of a radio or TV.

The Kennington Oval, venue for the 14th match of the Prudential World Cup, has more beanie hats, dreadlocks and shirts with shades of red, green and gold than turbans, baldies and pot bellies in attendance; including Mintu Bhatia and his nouveau-riche Southall friends. Not because Croydon is 6 miles and Southall 14 miles from the Oval. It's largely because everybody loves backing a winner. The Croydonites are here in large numbers to egg the World Champions on. The Southallians fear the worst; hence the small turnout. Manchester, six days ago, was a fluke. Both sets know.

Somewhere in between them sits an Indian. Indian-Indian. Not Southall Indian. Or Indian from anywhere in Blighty. Rajdeep Sardesai has travelled from Bombay. Not to watch this match specifically. He's been here for over a month now. Playing club cricket as a quasi-professional. Rajdeep's father is the famous test cricketer Dilip Sardesai, known as the Renaissance Man of Indian cricket after his stunning performance in India's historic test series wins in the West Indies and England 12 years ago. The son is keen to follow in his father's footsteps. Hence, this four-month exposure trip to England. Eighteen-year-old Rajdeep is a diehard West Indian fan. As are most cricket fans his age. Not only are the Calypso Kings the best team on the planet by a country mile, they are also the coolest. Their firebrand cricket is loved and appreciated the world over. Their swagger, both on and off the field, is what sets them apart as superstars and darlings of fans and promoters alike. Rajdeep has made the 70-mile journey, hustled a match ticket, just to watch the 'kings of cricket' in action. And maybe recite a prayer or two for his countrymen while he's there.

Inside the Indian dressing room, Sunil Valson sits nervously. He's one of the only two players in the 14-member squad who's not taken the field in the tournament yet. Roger Binny is undergoing a last-moment fitness test on the ground. Could this be the day the Delhi seamer makes his India debut?

Cheeka has now entangled his legs in the extra-wide bottom hem of his bell-bottoms and has fallen, face first, on the dressing room floor, tearing the crotch point of his trousers in the process. Not unusual for the uncoordinated Srikkanth. His teammates can't help but guffaw at his latest contretemps. With the exception of Valson. Binny has cleared the fitness test, he's just learnt.

Kapil reads out the playing XI. Gavaskar finds his name missing. He's feeling 100 per cent and ready to go. Only, no one asked him about his fitness.

The Indian team has taken the field. Greenidge and Desmond Haynes are out to bat. Ayaz hasn't noticed Gavaskar's absence. He's busy admiring the iconic ground's honours board. It has the names of several of his heroes engraved on wood, including Gavaskar's, for his 221 four years ago, the highest score by an Indian at the Oval.

17 for 1. Greenidge is the first wicket to fall. Bowled Kapil, caught Vengsarkar. 'Caught who? Vengsarkar?' Now it has struck Ayaz! Gavaskar is not playing for the second time in a row. 'Maybe a minor tiff has turned into a full-blown fight,' Ayaz's well-trained, ever-ticking journalistic mind is telling him.

Viv Richards has revenge on his mind. Unarguably the most destructive batsman of his generation, he is still smarting from that loss six days ago. Nonchalantly chewing Beech-Nut Gum, he steps back, moves away from the line of the ball, swings his bat, and sends the red cherry skywards. Sandeep Patil, at short third man, with a smirk on his face as if to say 'I knew it', watches the ball sail over the point boundary and settle on the third floor of the Oval pavilion.

Two minutes later – that's how long it has taken to retrieve the ball – a determined Roger Binny is running in to bowl the next delivery. This time he's better prepared. Expecting Viv to have another go at it, he rolls his index finger over the ball at the time of its release. The batsman repeats his action from a ball before. Only this time, the ball is travelling marginally slower. Viv has got this wrong. The change of speed has upset his timing. The ball has ballooned up in the air. It's heading towards Patil. Rajdeep has his jaws open. Ayaz has paused his typing. Mintu has stopped chomping on his fried fish. The third man needs to take a few steps forward. Quickly. He doesn't. The ball hits the turf.

Viv is alive. Binny wants to kill Patil.

Kapil, looking at Patil, has his hands pointing skyward. The universal gesture for 'what the bloody hell happened?' 'Who would have thought that *the* Viv Richards would make a mistake?' Patil mutters under his breath. The game carries on.

Richards is now more aware. Conscious of not allowing retribution to overpower prudence. Mixing caution with aggression, he's added 101 runs with Haynes. The West Indies are 118 for 1.

Bob Marley's latest single is blasting out of an old boom box, planted on the shoulder of a spectator in the lower stands – a preserve for the plain folks. The song is 'Buffalo soldier'. Haynes is out. Viv Richards is soldiering on. He's now on 86. That marks his 2000th run in one-day cricket. No one seems to have realized this. Including Richards. The fans are swaying to reggae in the stands, expecting another century from the Master Blaster.

One 6, six 4s, and 146 balls later, Viv Richards has accumulated 119 runs. At an uncharacteristic strike rate of well below 100. A restrained show by his high standards. But it has helped the West Indies finish with 282 at the end of their 60 overs. 20 more than what India managed when these sides last met less than a week ago.

Ayaz has met Srikkanth even before he can enter the changing room. As the two smokers often did. Innings break is as good a time as any to share a puff or two. Though, this time, Ayaz is hoping his mate, Cheeka – whom he first encountered as a university cricketer, playing a visiting English team, and has been a fan of his cavalier approach to cricket ever since – can share some other information too.

'Is there something happening between Sunny and Kaps?' the scribe wants to know.

'I don't know, da! He's been a bit quiet; that's all I've noticed,' is all the opening batsman can offer his friend at the moment.

'He's chosen not to play or they don't want him to play?'

'Nooo idea, re! I am not part of the team think tank. Okay, gotta rush,' says Srikkanth, and runs up the dressing room stairs. 'I'm the first one in, no.'

Srikkanth is also the first one out. As swiftly as he had run up the stairs to change, he's back in the dressing room after scoring 2 runs. Followed by his makeshift opening partner, Ravi Shastri, who's out for 6. Both victims to Andy Roberts. The early dismissals have been bittersweet for the openers. Bitter because they got out cheaply. Sweet because they are back without any serious injuries. The West Indian pace battery is breathing fire. Amarnath and Vengsarkar are at the crease. India are reeling at 21 for 2.

Clive Lloyd has tossed the ball to 25-year-old Malcolm Marshall. Vengsarkar being at the crease has a lot to do with it. They have a history, these two.

Circa 1978. The West Indies are touring India for a five-test series. The second test is in Bangalore. Malcolm Marshall is making his international debut. Batting first, the West Indies are 383 for 7. A healthy score by any standards. But the debutant is keen to impress. In the squad predominantly as an out-and-out quick bowler, the 20-year-old is determined to contribute with the bat too. The Indian spin trio of Bishan Singh Bedi, B.S. Chandrasekhar and Srinivasaraghavan Venkataraghavan aren't making it easy though. Vengsarkar's constant appealing after each ball he misses is making it worse. The Bombay batsman, two years Marshall's senior in international cricket, has identified an easy prey in the nervous debutant and is going in for the kill. Constant sledging is followed by vociferous appeals. Under pressure, umpire S. Kishen raises his index finger. Marshall is out, LBW to Chandra. The batsman, at first, stands his ground and then begins the long walk back to the pavilion. The young boy, not used to playing in front of such big crowds, has tears rolling down his cheeks. He feels cheated and humiliated. Minutes later, sitting in the dressing room, after a cold shower, he marks Vengsarkar as the main culprit. And vows revenge.

The Vengsarkar Vengeance is alive till date. Marshall remembers the taunts and ridicule like it was just yesterday.

Marley's 'Stir it up' is playing on the boom box. Loud in the stands, barely audible at the centre of the ground. Marshall has increased his pace and shortened his length. He is bowling at Vengsarkar, not to him. Vengsarkar is evading, not batting.

Watching his schoolmate, now teammate, nervously in the dressing room is Sandeep Patil, the next man in. He is padded up. But not quite ready to face up.

'Something's gotta give soon,' Ayaz has a sudden premonition. He can't sit still. Standing seems better. In the safe confines of the press box, of course. Behind a glass screen.

A screen is what Vengsarkar's helmet is missing. The blue shell – made of ABS plastic and high-density foam – is protecting his head all right, but the lack of a steel grill has his face exposed. Marshall bowls his umpteenth bouncer of the match. The sharp, rising delivery, clocking over 90 miles an hour, hits him on the chin. Vengsarkar is down for the count. Amarnath runs towards him. He knows what a Marshall bouncer to the chin feels like, having experienced it just a couple of months ago in Barbados; that ended with him being rushed to a hospital and receiving six stitches. The fielders have converged too. Marshall stays at the end of his follow through, expressionless. A few blades of grass have now turned red. The boom box has been paused. India's 12th man, Kirti Azad, rushes in. With a white handkerchief held to his chin, Vengsarkar is walking back. Retired hurt. The opposition's

Faoud Bacchus is carrying his helmet for him. Azad is carrying Vengsarkar. Sandeep Patil crosses them and takes strike. The sight of a batsman with blood oozing from his chin hasn't done the already low-on-confidence Patil much good. Marshall is at the top of his run-up, loaded, and ready to fire.

Bingo! Marshall has hit another target. The very first ball Patil has faced has hit him on his hand, torn his glove, and given him a deep cut.

Three beers down, Mintu Bhatia has a few choice words to say to the West Indian bowlers. He can be heard over the boom box. Which is now playing the 10-year-old classic 'Get up, stand up'. Bob Marley, of course.

That's exactly what Mohinder Amarnath is doing. Braving some seriously hostile bowling. It seems Messrs Roberts, Holding and Marshall are here with the intention of maiming the Indian batsmen. Amarnath has already endured a few nasty blows to his body. Yet, in the words of the great man Marley, he's standing up. As he's done on numerous occasions before. Why, when that Marshall bouncer gave him six stitches on the chin only two months ago, he came back from the hospital, washed the bloodstains off his shirt, and went out to bat at the fall of the next wicket. Only to be greeted with a bouncer from Holding. Which he hooked from under his freshly stitched chin for a boundary. He would go on to make 80, and pick up the Man of the Match award.

Once again, in the face of adversity, Amarnath, carrying his lucky red handkerchief, and with his T-shirt buttoned right up till his chin, is refusing to take a step back. He's gone past 51. His highest score in all of the 25 one-day matches he's played so far.

That's all there is for India to celebrate on the day. Kapil and his men have folded for 216, 66 short of the target. Amarnath alone has scored 80. Normal service has been restored. The West Indies are playing like the World Champions they are; India, with two humiliating losses in a row, are like the minnows that they really are.

The fans aren't surprised either. Mintu, Kulwant and Saran have joined the Caribbean party, ditching their beers for some rum and Coke. Rajdeep has boarded the train back to Sussex. Along with him, he's carrying a lifetime of memories, becoming an even bigger fan of the Windies than he already was.

Ayaz, observing the Indian dressing room balcony from the press box, is trying to read Gavaskar's face. The news from a nearby hospital is that Vengsarkar has received seven stitches on his face.

14

Tu(r)nbridge Wells

17 June 1983, London

Yashpal Sharma has woken up to an empty room. 'Where's Balwinder?' he wonders. The room in West Moreland Hotel isn't big enough to comfortably accommodate two people; especially with two large bags apiece. Which is why the Indian team has decided to keep kitbags and suitcases in the team bus at all times; only handbags, carrying just the bare necessities, are found in each room. Yashpal looks at the watch on his bedside table. It's 10 a.m. That explains where his roommate must be: at the breakfast table. And he's late! The team is scheduled to leave for practice at 10.30 a.m. sharp.

Yashpal has hardly slept. He was venting to Sandhu till the wee hours. India's two consecutive losses aside, Yashpal has been a bit disturbed the last few days – hurt at being pushed down the batting order. Especially after he did so well in the opening match against the West Indies, scoring a match-winning 89 and earning the Man of the Match award. Since then, he's been demoted to number 6 for three successive games, and has failed in all. Not a place where the senior pro wants to be. 'They are destroying my confidence,' is how the sentimental batsman had summed up his feelings last night. 'Don't worry; they must have a plan in mind,' is the best Sandhu could offer to pacify his roommate.

At 10.25, Yashpal is hurrying into the restaurant, screaming, 'I'm late, I'm late, I'm late!' He looks at the waitress nearest to the table he has sat down on. He has five minutes to pile on the calories before the team bus leaves for what promises to be a long and tiring day on the field. All three of his teammates at the table are through with their breakfast and are ready to leave. 'You aren't late, sir,' says the waitress, while turning a cup right side up and pouring him some hot, freshly brewed English tea. 'The breakfast buffet is on till 11a.m. What can I get you?'

Yashpal gives her a befuddled look. The waitress is wondering if she said something wrong. Before confusion reigns, Syed Kirmani, sitting at the same table, in his ever-polite tone, decodes Yashpal's Punjabi accent and saves the day: 'He told you what he wants for breakfast as soon as he walked in, ma'am. He'd like a fried "omelette" for breakfast, please.'

The Indian team is fried under the sun. This has been, as stated before, an unusually warm English summer. Today is one of those 30-degree days. Somehow, 30 degrees in England feels hotter than 30 degrees back home. Worse still, they've been practising for four hours at a stretch. On Kapil Dev's instructions. Strangely, not much time has been devoted to batting and bowling, as is the norm. Calisthenics and fielding drills are the focus for the day. The skipper has been relentless in his pursuit of a fitter, better fielding side all through this tournament.

The Indian team is in a precarious position at this stage of the tournament. They had an unbelievable start, winning their first two matches against the West Indies and Zimbabwe. But since then, they've tasted two defeats, to Australia and in the return leg against the West Indies; and two heavy defeats at that! From leading the group after two matches, they now sit in the third spot, out of a total of four; tied on points with Australia, but behind them in both run rate and the head-to-head comparison. With two matches to go, one of them against the mighty Aussies, India's chance of qualifying for the semi-final as the second team from the group is hanging by a thread. But that's not the only reason the captain is high-strung today.

Reams of broadsheet are being used to discuss the Gavaskar versus Kapil saga back home, the skipper has just learnt. Miles away, and without access to Indian newspapers, it's taken a couple of days for Kapil to realize the extent to which the controversy has escalated. Details of the case aside –

which is anyway scantily available to the media – Kapil is hurt at the narrative that's being pushed. He reckons it's the predominantly Bombay-based cricket media that's playing a partisan role in making Gavaskar the victim, and him the villain. The ever-prudent Man Singh can sense that something is troubling his skipper and pulls him aside, even as the rest of the team practises. 'You can't let a small matter like this affect the team's chances in a major tournament such as this!'

'You know there is no issue on my part at all. It is this Bombay press that has amplified this supposed "cold war". They can't fathom that the national team is being run by a non-Bombaywalla,' says an emotional Kapil in Hindi.

'Be that as it may, I only know one thing – nothing is bigger than the team, and you too know that better than anyone else. So, let them write, you do what's right.'

18 June 1983

Weaving through a crowd of prostitutes, inebriated men and vagabonds, in what is London's most seedy area, Ayaz has reached the entrance of King's Cross station, among the city's most-imposing structures. Named after King George IV, the Victorian-style building was designed more than a century ago and is now a part of the most-frequented public transport hub in the city. The main entrance is divided into two by a concrete tower in the centre, atop which sits a giant clock – also serving as the prime motif of the facade. Despite how large it is, Ayaz can't find a gap big enough to squeeze through the arched entrance. It's 9.30 a.m. – peak arrival time for those travelling to London for work. Adopting a dogged approach – the type shown by Gavaskar on a damp pitch in Jamaica against the West Indian quicks – he finally manages to worm his way through the oncoming crowd. The rush hasn't delayed him. There's plenty of time before his train to Tunbridge Wells – the venue of India's match today – departs. The 50-minute journey is sure to result in Ayaz reaching the ground well after the match has begun, but that's the best his tight budget can afford at the moment. Taking an expensive peak-hour train to reach the venue before the first ball is bowled isn't an option. A non-peak hour train, with a 50 per cent discount on the ticket, would have to suffice. Sitting in the station's central concourse, under an arched roof made of glass and supported by ribs of steel, which allow sunlight to filter in, Ayaz waits for his train to arrive. He's mulling over the team India will play for the crucial match today: Vengsarkar is ruled out, but who will replace him? Will Gavaskar be brought back? Or will the captain go with another all-rounder, Kirti Azad – one of the only two players in the squad not to have made his World Cup debut yet?

But for sure, it's a World Cup debut for the quaint, sleepy little Nevill Ground. In fact, it's the first-ever international match that this local village ground is hosting; and it isn't even the premier ground in its own county, Kent. Though, according to renowned sportswriter, E.W. Swanston, 'It remains a strong contender for the most delectable English cricket ground.'

In the basement of the only concrete structure on the ground, which is also serving as the Indian team's dressing room for the day, sits the team's 'tour selection committee', comprising the captain, vice captain and manager. The trio is in the middle of an animated discussion, even as the rest of the team warms up on the field.

There is a steady crowd building up. The locals are settling down on the hillocks skirting the boundary rope, many bringing their own chairs from home. The small 70-yard boundary promising a more inclusive experience for the spectators. But for those at home, 'tough luck'. There aren't any cameras on this ground to relay live pictures. None to even record it for a highlights package later. The BBC has two very sumptuous cricket matches on its menu already. The broadcaster's programme for the day reads: 'The four most powerful cricketing countries in the world do battle. WEST INDIES meet AUSTRALIA at Lord's, and Old Trafford will witness a vital result with only one match remaining before the semi-finals. Commentators: Old Trafford: RICHIE BENAUD, TONY GREIG, FRANK TYSON; Lord's: JIM LAKER, TOM GRAVENEY, TED DEXTER.'

For the powers that be at the BBC, India versus Zimbabwe doesn't merit a camera crew.

But does Gavaskar merit a place in the playing XI? That is the question the stakeholders of Indian cricket seem to be more bothered about at the moment. The man himself doesn't know. He is sitting near the stairs of the dressing room, in open view. Kapil walks past him, heading to the centre of the field where the opposition captain, Duncan Fletcher, is waiting. The freshly minted, gold-coloured, one-pound coin is tossed up in the air. Queen Elizabeth II and the royal coat of arms are taking turns to face the two captains standing below, who don't know yet which side will fall face first. Kapil is hoping it's the coat of arms; he's chosen the queen, after all.

'Sunny, all the best,' shouts a scribe, holding the team sheet in his hand, from the tent pitched next to the main pavilion – the makeshift press box for the day. Before Gavaskar can turn around and react, 'Sunil, pad up, we are batting,' says Kapil, as he walks down the stairs into the dressing room. The skipper seems to have called correctly... At the toss.

With a healthy dose of expat Indians sprinkled behind the white picket fence that rims the boundary, Sunil Gavaskar takes guard.

Peter Rawson releases the ball, allowing it to float rather than hit the pitch hard. The delivery bounces, and then moves sharply off the pitch. Gavaskar pokes his bat at it, but misses the line completely. The ball has come to rest in the gloves of wicketkeeper, Dave Houghton. The crowd lets out a collective sigh. This is unfamiliar territory for Gavaskar. Not the conditions, the quality of bowling or even his enigmatic form – he's come through much tougher times during his 12 years in international cricket. But for a man who is a stickler for detail and process, he's been discombobulated by not having his customary 20 minutes in isolation – a routine that helps him prepare ahead of every knock he plays. The next ball hits him on his pads, dead in front of the stumps. He's walking back, with no runs to show.

At the other end, his opening partner refuses to take cognizance of the tough conditions on offer. As always, looking to dominate, Srikkanth has pulled Kevin Curran. Only, he hasn't gotten hold of the ball. The top edge flies to long on. Iain Butchart at mid-on makes a dash for it. A 30-metre sprint later, he has the cherry in his hand.

'Unfortunately... India have lost both its openers... And neither have managed to trouble the scorers,' announces a feeble Farokh Engineer, a former India cricketer and the radio commentator for this match, a man usually high on energy.

Having seen stations like Petts Wood, High Brooms and Chislehurst go by, Ayaz has arrived at his destination. A mile-long walk from Tunbridge Wells station, along the cobblestone streets, he's reached the Nevill Ground, which is nestled between residential houses and a thick row of Himalayan birch trees. It's a little after 11 in the morning when Ayaz enters the ground to a thunderous cheer. But he isn't that famous yet, he knows. 'Must be an acknowledgement of some great Indian feat,' he reckons. He looks up at the Indian players sitting in the pavilion for a clue while making his way to the press tent. Sullen faces are all he can see from 10 metres away. He spots a familiar face in the row closest to him. The maestro is sitting there, sipping his third pint of lager for the morning, stroking his moustache, lost in thought. 'What's up, Vishy?' asks Ayaz. 'Don't worry, it'll be all fine,' replies Gundappa Viswanath. The out-of-favour India batsman is here as a mere spectator. Ayaz looks over his shoulder and can see Sandeep Patil heading back to the pavilion. He's been caught by the wicketkeeper, off Curran. Instinctively, Ayaz tilts his neck skyward. The old, gigantic manual scoreboard at long on, flanked by a well-cropped row of hedges, reads 9 for 4. 'Mohinder Amarnath's inside edge was grabbed by the wicketkeeper just a short while ago,' he's informed by Viswanath.

Yashpal, now promoted to number five, has been joined by the Indian skipper, who looks rather bemused, in the middle. Ayaz, sitting alongside one of the finest Indian batsmen to have ever played the game, is wondering what he will write in his match report if India is all out for 40 or 50.

Five women, looking chic in their Indian attire, bunched together in the pavilion seating area, are cursing themselves. The first match they watch live at this World Cup and their spouses are having a terrible time in the middle. They arrived in England just a day ago. A pit stop of sorts. In a few days, they'll be off to the USA for a series their husbands are scheduled to participate in.

Zimbabwe are participating in their very first World Cup. Dubbed as the weakest team in the tournament, alongside India, they shocked Australia in their opening match. Much like India, who upset the West Indies in their opening encounter. Today, both teams are playing to stay alive in the tournament. A loss would mean the end of the semi-final dream. A dream indeed. Zimbabwe's rise in the shorter format of the game hasn't happened overnight. Once recognized the world over as a group of beer guzzlers, they've gone through a 360-degree transformation under captain Duncan Fletcher. Their preparation for this tournament was hard and tough. Almost boot camp-like. Ian Robertson, an ex-South African rugby player, was entrusted with the responsibility of training them. And train them he did, employing some of the most difficult drills, involving heavy weights and obstacles. Baseball pitchers were used to get the batsmen used to the extra pace. As a result, the Zimbabwe team that arrived in England was fitter than even their rugby counterparts. And they are the best fielding side on the planet by a distance.

Looks like Yashpal's change in batting position hasn't changed his luck with the bat. He's Rawson's third scalp of the day, and wicketkeeper Houghton's third catch.

India's wicketkeeper, on the other hand, is sitting in the dressing room – below the level of the playing field – oblivious to what's happening in the centre. Wearing only a towel around his waist, a slice of toast in one hand and a cup of tea in the other, he's all set to hit the shower, when, 'Hey, Kiri, pad up,' comes a voice from outside. 'Someone's surely joking,' the Indian wicketkeeper, not used to getting a chance to bat at all in one-day cricket, tells himself. A minute later, the voice comes again, 'Kiri, what are you doing, man? Put your gear on!' Kirmani, now convinced it's not a joke, walks up to the window to peep at the scoreboard. India: 17 for 5! His lower jaw has dropped to the ground, and so has his towel.

A few Indian fans too seemed to have thrown in their towels. A bunch, sitting in the pavilion that shares a roof with the Indian dressing room, who were cheering for their team just a short while ago, have begun to heckle them. The players who were sitting in the veranda outside the dressing room have decided to return indoors.

Former BCCI president, and the current president of the Bombay Cricket Association, S.K. Wankhede, is witnessing the collapse live. He quickly sends a message across to his driver not to leave the stadium. His earlier plans of leaving only in the evening may now have to be changed. 'Sir should be done soon,' a member of the ground pantry staff tells the driver.

Kapil has walked halfway to the pavilion to meet the next batsman in. Roger Binny is walking gingerly. He's nervous and his mind is clouded with self-doubt. 'We have plenty of overs to go; let's just take our time, play a few balls, take singles, no boundaries,' are Kapil's first words to him.

Fifty miles south of Tunbridge Wells, in Arundel, Rajdeep Sardesai, playing for his club Worthing, is trying to conquer his own self-doubts. Like India against Zimbabwe, his team too finds itself in a sticky situation, having lost their first four wickets for just 20 runs. Rajdeep is the lone quasi-professional in a team made up of truck drivers, plumbers and gardeners, and, hence, must shoulder the responsibility of getting all the runs today. The trouble is, born and raised on the slow and low tracks of west India, the 18-year-old has been having a torrid time of late; struggling to score runs in the swinging conditions of England since the time he's arrived here, just over a month ago. Captaining Bombay schools and starring for West Zone schools now seems like memories from another lifetime.

Here comes another swinging delivery... And that's another play-and-a-miss from Rajdeep.

Roger Binny has had to endure a few plays-and-misses of his own during his 30-ball stay. But, more importantly, he's still at the crease. He and Kapil have helped India cross the 50-run mark. It's been a tough 40-ball innings for Kapil too. An inherently aggressive batsman, he's had to curb his natural instincts and keep the ball on the ground; nudging it around for mostly 1s and 2s. At least now, this won't be the lowest total by any team in a World Cup. Canada hold that dubious distinction when they managed just 45 versus England four years ago.

Zimbabwe's two wreckers-in-chief, Curran and Rawson, have been given a break by Duncan Fletcher. Both have bowled eight overs apiece and still have four more overs each to complete their respective quotas. But the Zimbabwe skipper feels it's best to give them a breather now – he wants to save them for the latter part of the Indian innings. For now, Fletcher has brought himself on from one end, while Iain Butchart bowls from the other.

Kapil senses an opportunity. He starts to play a few strokes now. Not every shot is heading in the direction he wants it to – the ball is still moving around a fair bit – but he's not complaining. His effort at trying to send a ball over midwicket sends it racing towards the third-man boundary instead. 'A 4 is a 4 is a 4,' he tells himself.

Two gentlemen have walked up to Dave Ellman-Brown, chairman of the Zimbabwe Cricket Union. They claim to be the local organizers, and are worried the match is turning into a fiasco. This is the first international match this ground is hosting, and the only one this World Cup. If this gets over by lunchtime, who knows if they'll ever get another match of any relevance to host? Brown's not too impressed with their reading of the game. 'This is cricket, gents. Things don't take too long to change.'

The two organizers aren't very impressed with Brown either. The ball has caught Roger Binny on his pads. The umpire has given him his marching orders. It's the end of a patient 60-run stand. At 77 for 6, the Indian batting is ailing.

In the hospital, listening to the proceedings on the radio, Vengsarkar is wondering if he could have made the difference today. 'Umm… On second thoughts… Not really' – Ravi Shastri is the latest to head back to the pavilion – 'Who would I have batted with anyway?' he thinks. It is now 78 for 7.

Farokh has left his position at the commentary box and a bowl full of crisps to head into the Indian dressing room next door. 'Come on, guys, just give Kapil company,' he screams in his commentator-like stirring tone, even as Madan Lal walks out to join Kapil. 'Even 150 on this pitch could give you a fighting chance.'

The news of India's collapse has reached far and wide. The BBC – which wasn't too interested in covering this insignificant game to begin with – now wants to send a camera crew from London to interview the Zimbabwe players soon after the win, their second victory in their World Cup debut. The TV crew has contacted Dave Ellman-Brown through the Nevill Ground pavilion's landline. He tells them the same thing that he told the local organizers a short while ago: 'This game isn't over yet.'

With only three wickets remaining, Kapil has begun to realize that he may not have too many overs left to bat. He must cut loose. And with an off-spinner bowling, he doesn't need another invitation. But he faces a dilemma. The match is being played on a pitch at the very edge of the square; which means one boundary is immense, allowing the batsman to even run 3 for a shot that doesn't have the legs to cross the boundary; while on the other side, you can either run a single or very easily earn a boundary. Kapil must make his choice. Either hit John Traicos with the spin on the leg side – the safer option – and collect 2s and 3s. Or hit him against the spin – the tougher shot to play – but collect a 4 or a 6.

The calm, Buddha-like Kapil has picked the middle path: choosing the easier option of playing with the spin, but also hit it hard enough to fetch him the maximum. Now, an off-the-legs flick has travelled over midwicket, the boundary rope, the temporary tents, the neatly manicured hedges, the tall birch trees, and landed on the adjoining farm. Too far to be found and retrieved. A replacement ball has been brought in.

No balls have been lost in Arundel though, but Rajdeep seems to have found his confidence. He's bailed his club team out by scoring a gritty 60. Biding your time at the crease until the ball gets old and stops swinging is the trick in succeeding in these English conditions, he's realized; the runs will follow.

Kapil is now picking most of his runs by hitting towards the longer boundary. Still not being over-adventurous though. Slashing the ball off the back foot, over covers, is the only aerial shot he's playing. The new ball seems a bit docile too. Meanwhile, Madan Lal has collected 17 runs of his own.

Fletcher needs to wrest the initiative back from India. Kevin Curran is brought back into the attack. On cue, he delivers a wicket to his skipper. Kapil watches as yet another partner abandons him. The 62-run partnership has ended.

At 140 for 8, Syed Kirmani, trousers firmly around his waist, has walked out to join him. 'I will just give you strike; you do your thing. But rest assured, before I perish, I'll ensure that the opposition is dead and buried,' the senior pro tells his skipper before facing his first ball.

Plan B is in action now. Kapil is to look for boundaries in the first five balls of the over and then a single off the last ball to ensure he keeps the strike. Kapil's trademark Nataraja pull has now sent the ball racing towards the square-leg boundary. It comes to rest after hitting the sponsor hoarding behind the boundary rope. The red billboard, made of tin, has 'Celcon

Building Blocks' written on it. Kapil and Kirmani are now rebuilding India's challenge, block by block.

Behind the billboards, square of the pitch on both sides, is a row of spectators sitting on chairs are that they've brought from home. Those who haven't are either standing behind the chairs or are sprawled on the hillocks rimming the ground, most of them bare chested. The English summer is in full bloom. The sun is bright. Further back, there's smoke rising from a host of barbeques spread across the ground. Each surrounded by a group of peckish cricket fans. Mintu and friends aren't one of them. They've got their home-made shalgam ka saag and makki ki roti packed in neat steel tiffin boxes. It goes well with the barley and hops.

It's time for lunch – as scheduled, at the end of the 35th over. Kapil's watchful 70* has been interrupted. Maybe he needs a break to soak in what's just transpired. Maybe some stimulation too, from his teammates. Twenty-five overs still remain. But there are no remains of the Indian team. Kapil and Kirmani have walked into an empty dressing room. The rest of the gang have moved back into the open area in the pavilion, now safe from the heckling fans after the semblance of recovery being shown by the team they support. And much safer from what they perceive must be a fuming captain. They've assessed this well. Kapil has gone into the adjoining room, reserved for lunch, to look for his colleagues. He may not need a drink with his lunch today to wash it down his throat. He'll just have to gulp down his anger, he's realized upon finding another empty room.

Refuelled, the skipper is channelizing his fury to drive himself, and the ball. Two have just flown over the boundary rope. He's into the 90s now.

Here comes another one. Third in a row. The ball is heading for the clouds. Moving more vertical than horizontal. Can it cross the boundary? Grant Paterson is settling under it, at the edge of the boundary. He seems to have a measure of the height, drift and speed at which it's hurtling down. He has joined his hands and cupped his palms in front of his chest. Eyes on the ball. Thud! The cherry has landed safely. On the turf. Missing the moist and supple nook – made from human skin with high eumelanin levels – that had been hurriedly prepared for it.

The proceedings in Arendel have come to a halt, in the meanwhile. There are a total of six Indian-origin players in the two teams competing this afternoon, apart from Rajdeep. A radio has been quickly arranged for. Both teams have huddled around it. Kapil Dev is on to something special, they suspect.

The commentators agree. 'This is a very, very special knock by Kapil Dev... The first one-day century of his career... And under the circumstances, without doubt, one of the best one-day knocks by an Indian,' is how an exuberant Farokh Engineer is describing what he's seeing; personally pleased at

India having gone past the 150-run target he'd set for them when they were 78 for 7.

Wankhede's driver is still standing next to the car, wondering what happened to his boss who was expected to leave more than an hour and a half ago.

There are still 11 overs to go. Kapil Dev is in the mood. He has called for a new bat. One with tapering shoulders. It's in vogue. A baseball bat disguised as a cricket willow.

Syed Kirmani doesn't need to change his bat. Or his approach. His singles are doing the job. He is playing his part to perfection. So is the rest of the Indian team. They've not moved since lunch. All glued to their chairs. Some by choice, others by order. 'No one moves from where they are sitting, lest they bring bad luck and force Kapil's dismissals,' are superstitious Man Singh's strict instructions. Cheeka is standing with his wife, Vidya, under a tree, a couple of yards away from the pavilion. The shade from the pavilion roof, coupled with a breeze, is making him cold. He wants to return to the dressing room. He's been wanting that for half an hour now. 'Nothing doing, no moving!' is the common consensus in the Indian camp. The one most desperate to move is Kirti Azad. He's been holding on to his excreta for the last five overs. 'Do it here for all I care,' is all that Man Singh can offer to him in terms of relief.

Kapil, in turn, has had a moment or two of relief. Not everything is hitting the sweet spot of his new bat. Rare mishits have landed in no man's land and allowed him a couple of runs; a few edges have sped to the short boundary. In the process, India have crossed the psychological 200-run mark. Suddenly, like the blooming rhododendron flowers scattered across the ground, the Indian innings is looking in the pink of its health. Rawson and Curran, who looked unplayable at the start, are now seeing the ball fly off Kapil's bat. Their figures ruined in the final spell of the match. Iain Butchart, with his gentle, right-arm medium, is the only one keeping a rampaging Kapil in check – by aiming his yorkers consistently at his legs. Yet, neither he nor anyone else from the Zimbabwe team can stop the Haryana Hurricane from setting a new world record. Soon, he's gone past Glenn Turner's 171 that was scored eight years ago – the highest score in a one-day game until today.

Sixteen boundaries, six of some of the biggest sixers ever, and 181 minutes later, Kapil finishes with the finest 175 runs ever scored on a cricket field. His strike rate of 126.81 is rarer still. The 126-run unbroken stand between him and Syed Kirmani is also a new record for the ninth wicket. From 17 for 5, India have reached a barely believable 266.

Kapil and Kirmani are walking off to a raucous applause. A former BCCI president, spouses of Indian as well as of opposition players, all adding to the thunderous ovation. The Little Master Gundappa Viswanath is on his feet. The other Little Master Sunil Gavaskar has walked on to the playing field, offering Kapil a glass of water. The rest of the Indian team is hooting from the pavilion. Except Kirti. He's been allowed to leak water.

Seventy years ago, the pavilion at this very ground was set on fire by the suffragettes. Today, Kapil is walking into the same structure, now refurbished with fresh wood and cement, having set the tournament ablaze.

Farokh has caught up with Dave Houghton as the Zimbabweans walk off the field. 'Kapil's outstanding knock aside, we believe this is a beautiful batting pitch and we should be able to chase down 266 comfortably,' the wicketkeeper tells BBC radio.

'These guys struggled against the swing of Binny and Madan in that opening match against India in Leicester,' remarks Rajdeep, sitting next to the radio. 'Exactly, they barely went past 150 on that occasion,' concurs one of his teammates, an Indian-origin off-spinner. 'That was a different pitch, boys. 266 here may not be tough,' observes Derek Symonds, Rajdeep's local guardian and Worthing Cricket Club's manager for the match. 'Anyway, lads, let's get back on the field and get done with our game. Hurry up!'

Zimbabwe's opening pair seems to be in a hurry. Brown and Paterson have put together a solid 44-run stand. Paterson, in particular, seems to have taken a liking towards Madan Lal and Co. His 23 include four hits to the boundary. Trying his best to make up for dropping Kapil, perhaps.

Ayaz has his catch of the day. The biggest story of the World Cup. A once-in-a-lifetime innings, he knows. Now, it's time for the fan in him to make way for the professional that has been sent across continents to cover the World Cup.

His boss in Bombay wants an account of Kapil's knock more than a report on the entire match. 'That 175 is pretty much the entire match,' Ayaz has been reminded. His fingers are typing away furiously – the only thing quicker than Paterson's strike rate at the moment – expressing what he's just witnessed live. One thousand two hundred words later, he's done. Now is the tough bit. For all the scenic beauty of this small-town ground, it doesn't have a fax machine. Narrating the entire story over the phone will cost Ayaz as much as his entire trip. Telex remains his only option.

The umpire has no option but to give Paterson out. Binny has caught him on his pads, with a ball coming in, bang in front of the stumps. Before Paterson can even take his pads off in the dressing room, Jack Heron is run-out. Trying to run 2 when there was no more than 1.

Ayaz has come running into the telex operator's room. The process of retyping his story on the telex machine has begun.

Robin Brown's story in this match has ended. Trying to steal a single off a ball that's hit the striker Duncan Fletcher's leg has resulted in the sheet anchor being well short of his crease. The skipper's loud 'no' was of no avail.

The telex tape with a code for Ayaz's story is ready. The operator at Tunbridge Wells is dialling *Mid-Day*'s telex machine in Bombay. The two machines are connected. The coded tape is playing out. The machine in Bombay is decoding and printing a new coded sheet of paper simultaneously. The freshly printed sheet has been rushed to the office compositor. He's asked to key it in on hot metal.

Zimbabwe are 113 for 6. Farokh's commentary suggests that Indian bowlers haven't been at their best. At least not as good as they had been against the same team in Leicester, exactly a week ago. The inexperienced Africans have been found guilty of not playing it safe immediately after the fall of a wicket, even if that meant not scoring for a few overs.

The compositor's hot metal has released a proof. The proof is sent over to the subeditor. He's begun the correction process.

Kevin Curran has begun the correction process for Zimbabwe. Can this all-rounder do an encore of what another all-rounder did a couple of hours ago? With eight hits across the rope, he certainly looks in the mood. And in Butchart, and now Gerald Peckover, Zimbabwe seem to have found their Madan Lal and Kirmani.

The subeditor has finished with his corrections. The reworked script has been hurried back to the compositor. The corrected copy is being reprinted.

Correct and conventional up until now, Curran has finally played a false stroke. He has misjudged the pace of a long hop from Madan Lal, and the ball hits the shoulder of his bat, and lobs straight into Ravi Shastri's hands. Zimbabwe, 230 for 9. Still 37 behind.

Four and a half hours later, the final copy of a rare front-page sports story is done. So is the match. Zimbabwe falls 32 runs short of what looked like a sure-shot victory for them a few hours ago. Kapil, the man of the moment, the victorious captain, sinks down to his knees and bends to kiss the ground.

Vengsarkar has jumped out of his hospital bed. That he's injured, only his subliminal mind knows.

Those at the ground are still coming to terms with what they've just witnessed. Still unaware of the fact that they are, and will remain, the only privileged ones in the world to have seen 'The Kapil's Comet'. For all of BBC's 15 million recorded items – the largest broadcast archives in the world –

there will be no video record of one of the finest innings played on a cricket field.

Rajdeep can only imagine what it must be like in Tunbridge Wells at the moment. His teammates at Worthing have bought him a full jug of beer as they sit together at a local pub, celebrating their win in the Sussex league. On days he didn't score, Rajdeep has had to spend weekends sitting alone at home. But on occasions he did, like today, he can enjoy the company of his English teammates. It hasn't been easy for him to assimilate into English society. No matter how good a team man he can be, he'll always be an outsider, and he knows this. But there's new-found respect for Rajdeep within his team today. Not least because of the half-century he scored. He's scored a couple before. But more because of what Kapil and his team have managed to pull off. It's not a win for the Indian team alone, but a minor victory for an entire community that faces prejudice on a daily basis.

At the post-match press conference, Kapil is asked, 'Will India ever produce another Kapil Dev?'

'Never,' is the Indian skipper's reply. 'My mother old, father no more.'

15

Four for Begets Last Four

19 June 1983, London

'Who's Seve Ballesteros?' Kapil wants to know.

Sitting alongside Kapil, in the lobby of their London hotel, Man Singh has no idea. 'He might know,' says the team manager, spotting Ayaz talking to Sandeep Patil at the reception. He gesticulates for him to come over. Ayaz shakes Patil's hand and begins walking towards them.

Meanwhile, a surprised Man Singh asks, 'How did this name come up?'

'Nah, just this,' says Kapil, pointing towards an article in the *Times*. It reads: 'In Kapil Dev, India have the Seve Ballesteros of the game, a man capable of heroics.' It's written by John Woodcock, the celebrated cricket writer.

'You do know he's the best golfer on the planet, right?' Ayaz's rhetorical question is in response to the same article, having read it standing behind Man Singh. 'He won his second Masters title just two months ago, at the age of 26, would you believe it!'

Man Singh nods his head and exclaims, 'Wow! That's high praise. Isn't it?'

Kapil pouts and shrugs. He isn't sure.

Ayaz is. 'Of course, it's high praise! And that knock and win deserves nothing less. And that's not all, the English have a new name for you guys.' He takes the folded broadsheet that he's carrying and spreads it out on the table in front of Kapil and Man Singh. 'The *Daily Telegraph* is calling you guys Dev's Devils.'

'Ha ha ha…' Man Singh can't help but allow his belly to shake, unrestrained. 'It's only taken them five matches to go from Underdogs to Dev's Devils.'

Kapil just smirks. 'I'll leave you two to it,' he says, as he heads up to his room. The Devil, clearly, isn't interested in the details. But Man Singh and Ayaz are – in the minute details of the run rate. The current group standings offer much food for thought. Lunch is ordered. This may take a while. For starters, the West Indies, with four wins in five games have 16 points, and are the only team from Group B to have qualified for the semi-final. Par for the course. Zimbabwe are left deserted at the bottom of the table – four points from five matches – and are out of the reckoning. That leaves India and

Australia. Scheduled to play each other tomorrow. A virtual quarter-final. Both teams are hungry for a win. A win for India will take them to their first-ever World Cup semi-final. But if they make a meal of it, Australia will finish level on 12 points. 'What then?' Man Singh is not sure. 'The better run rate decides the last four.' Ayaz knows. There are only four tissue papers now on the table. The rest have been used by two sets of greasy hands. The same hands are at work again. Wielding the pen this time. Scribbling complex mathematical scenarios. Until the last paper is covered with ink. The semi-final puzzle still remains unsolved. Man Singh allows himself a deep burp. 'Forget this, let's just focus on winning the bloody game,' is the conclusion he's reached. 'A win against Australia?' Ayaz finds this difficult to swallow, the hiding by the same opposition exactly a week ago still fresh in his mind. But on second thoughts, 'Swallows and summers do go well together,' he concludes inside his head.

The bookmakers too have this last match between these two teams in mind. The odds on offer reflect that. 60:40 in favour of Australia. Despite India having won more games than Hughes and Co. so far.

The bookmaker's slip finds itself in a homemaker's hands. Sarla Parekh was sifting through her husband's wardrobe, looking for the gold-plated watch, when she stumbled upon this receipt, safely tucked away in the locked drawer, hidden behind her husband's shirts. She planned on wearing the watch for an interview at a nearby shoe store. Wanting to look her best. The store is looking for a part-time saleswoman. Sarla is desperately looking for a job. The last few days have been tough on the Parekh family. The 14 days her husband's shop had to remain shut has taken its toll on their finances. The refurbishment costs that followed have exhausted their meagre savings. The mortgage for their house and shop are due. The Parekhs could do with the extra money that comes from a part-time job.

Jiten Bhai, back from a full day's work, is sitting at the dinner table, alongside his two kids. He is unable to answer the questions being asked of him. Sarla can't digest the fact that her husband could, first, lie – about not getting any compensation from the insurance company – and then, callously spend that money on a silly bet, in the midst of a financial crisis at home. The catechizing process has seen Sarla go through four stages – anxiety, hysteria, choking and weeping, in that order. She leaves the table. The food on her plate untouched. Pooja follows her mother into the bedroom. Ten-year-old Nilesh takes a bite of his poori after dipping it in some hot aamras. He's waited 240 seconds for this – the time it took his mother to go through her full range of emotions. His father sits stupefied. He has lost his appetite. Guilt is eating him from within. 'What was I thinking?' he asks himself. The man, in the mirror that Sarla holds, has no answers.

20 June 1983, Chelmsford, Essex

There are reports in the media of infighting within the Australian team. 'Nothing new,' Kapil tells himself. It's been a theme throughout the tournament. Yet, the same opposition pummelled them just a week ago. And who knows it better than the skipper who ended up on the wrong side of that 162-run defeat. 'But this looks serious,' Kapil is beginning to realize. David Hookes has walked out for the toss instead of Kim Hughes. 'Hughes is out because of a thigh strain,' says the official statement. There's no Dennis Lillee in the playing XI either. Dropped for his wicket-less performance in the defeat against the West Indies two days ago? There's no official word on that. India have chosen to bat. Kapil didn't hesitate in deciding. The 162-run demoralizing defeat against the same team, while chasing, just eight days ago, is still fresh in his mind.

'Boys, good news! Captain scored 50 match before not playing today!' Kapil's announcement elicits blank stares from everyone in the dressing room. 'Lillee don't play in Trent Bridge, don't play today also.' More blank stares. Kirti Azad has slipped behind Kapil, sensing plenty more catches coming his way. 'You wanted four, Yashpal? You are four today.' Kirti guessed right. Kapil is at his lucid best. 'Seniors, any more ideas?' In between the giggles, the astute Gavaskar has an observation. 'Last match against them, we bowled short. We need to pitch it up and confuse the batsman which way it will swing, and Roger, with his ability to swing the ball both ways, can be our man.' Amarnath and Kirmani concur. 'If bowler don't know which way ball will swing, how will batsman know?' says Kapil, letting out a loud guffaw. The dressing room can't hide its mirth. Except Binny. He's can't find humour in Kapil's facetious remark. Seeing vexation writ large on Binny's face, Amarnath chips in to swing the conversation in another direction: 'Come on, guys, let's do this! It's do or die! Stay in the tournament or go home!'

Geoff Lawson takes Dennis Lillee's place in the playing XI. Ken MacLeay has replaced skipper Kim Hughes. Not surprising. MacLeay had, after all, picked up six wickets the last time the two teams met. But a bowler replacing a batsman is perhaps a reflection of how suspect their bowling has been leading up to this game.

Luckily for the Kangaroos, their pace spearhead, arguably the quickest bowler on the planet, Jeff Thomson, is in the mood. On a bright, hot day, he's running in with purpose, bending his back to generate as much pace as his 33-year-old body allows him to. India are soon 65 for 3. Thommo has packed up Srikkanth and Amarnath; Hogg has accounted for Gavaskar. Time for India to adopt a cautious approach and dig in their heels at the crease? Don't tell Sandeep Patil that. The hard-hitting Bombaywalla doesn't have a single defensive bone in his body. His 30 comes off 25 balls. But that's all. No further. MacLeay has him walking back to the pavilion. Yashpal is on a personal mission. Eager to prove he's senior enough, responsible enough to bat at the top of the order. This is his second World Cup. The Punjab batsman came here four years ago. His biggest contribution was to carry drinks as the 12th man in all three matches India played. He knows there isn't another World Cup in his career. This is it. 40 runs off 40 balls is his contribution. That's the maximum number of runs an Indian batsman has scored for the day. There is no rearguard action from Kapil Dev. But then, there's no collapse either. Kirti Azad could have collapsed. Attempting to rile up Jeff Thomson with indecorous gestures. 'I will break your f*cking head,' is the fast bowler's response. It's not the first time in his career that he has said this to a batsman. Madan Lal, at the other end, doesn't know what to make of Kirti's imprudence. 'What the hell are you doing? You know what this mad man is capable of.' 'Don't worry, this is his last over; that's why I am fingering him.' Kirti negotiates the next two bouncers, head and fingers intact. Not Thommo, but Lawson eventually gets him for 15. Like Kirti, each of India's 11 players have notched up double figures. Except two: numbers 1 and 11. Dev's Devils are all out for 247, 25 balls left unused. Extras are the second-highest contributors to India's total: 37 in all.

Australia, even without their skipper, are odds-on the favourites to get home, and knock India out of the tournament in the process. The pitch is a featherbed, pundits at the ground reckon. At 46 for 1, Australia are proving them right. Cruising towards the target effortlessly. The 16th over sees the introduction of Roger Binny, of 'don't-know-which-way-the-ball-will-swing' fame. Bowling with the press box – a glass cabin above the sight screen – behind him, the seamer is putting on a show. In three overs – 16th, 18th, 20th – he has reduced Australia to 52 for 4. Bowling seam up, he's been hitting all the right places consistently. The wise bunch in the press box reckons his gentle medium pace seems best suited to this kind of wicket. The opposition batsmen can't seem to read his in-dippers. Bowled, caught behind, caught and bowled are how he has got his scalps so far. Madan Lal is doing more of the same from the other end. Australia are soon 79 for 7. Roger's 4 for 29 and Madan's 4 for 20 have bundled out Australia for a mere 129, 118 short of the target. Roger Michael Humphrey Binny is the Man of the Match. He doesn't seem angry. And he's not feeling vindicated either. There's visible joy on his chevron-styled moustache-laden face. India, a team that had won just a solitary match in two previous editions of the tournament, are now World Cup semi-finalists.

16

Lost in Translation

21 June 1983, London

The ever-buoyant Mintu Bhatia has an extra spring in his step today. He's wrapping up the pending work at his restaurant and heading home, leaving the manager to deal with the evening rush. The plan is to reach Manchester – a four-hour drive from his home in Southall – by dinner time. He can't wait to see India take on England in the semi-final of a World Cup. The match starts in a little over 18 hours. But that's not the only thing he's kicked about. His wife called. Harry is home early. He wants to go for the game too. Some quality father–son time is all Mintu can envision at the moment. A rarity these days. What with him busy with his businesses, and his son busy fraternizing with the local lads. 'Oh, imagine sitting together, sharing a beer, cheering on our team, Dad and son,' Mintu's mind is racing.

Harry, with his long locks tied into a ponytail, is packing his rucksack when Mintu enters home. 'Oye! You are ready early. There's still time, *bachaa*, we'll leave only when Saran and Kulwant uncle are here. They'll take another hour, I guess.'

'What!' says Harry, not looking at his father, still busy packing his bag. 'Who said I am coming with you?'

'But your mom called…'

'And said what? I'm going with my mates, Dad.'

'Oh…' is Mintu's immediate reaction. Then, after a brief pause, 'No problem, see you at the game then,' sounding a bit dispirited unlike a few seconds ago.

'I don't think so, Dad,' says Harry nonchalantly.

'What do you mean? You aren't going to watch the match?'

'Of course I am; but I'd be sitting with my fellow English fans, seeing your India go down!' He sniggers as he gets ready to leave.

Mintu can only watch with a forced smile on his face as Harry picks up the keys for the red convertible and shuts the main door behind him.

The door of Man Singh's hotel room in Manchester is wide open. The players are trickling in. The official team meeting ahead of the semi-final is about to begin. Once everyone is inside, Man Singh lays down the agenda. The squad is informed that the Indian national broadcaster Doordarshan has taken the last-minute decision to telecast the semi-final live. Clearly, no one back home expected their team to reach this far, hence this last-minute *jugaad*. The final will also be beamed live, irrespective of whether India makes it or not. The announcement is met with nods of approval from the players. For the moment though, the manager wants his team to focus on his TV screen. He's playing a clip from a BBC programme that he recorded last evening. The programme is counting down to the impending India versus England semi-final. A member of the English team, Graeme Fowler, is the expert in the studio. But even after 10 minutes, there's no mention of India at all. The entire conversation is about England versus the West Indies. Can England beat the defending world champions? Can England handle the West Indies pace battery? For the hosts, it seems, the India game is nothing more than a walkover, only for England to meet the West Indies in the final.

Man Singh walks over to the large central table in his hotel suite. Picks up a bunch of newspapers. Turns off the tube. Reads the headlines aloud. The *Guardian*'s cricket reporter seems crestfallen, as is evident from his prematch report: 'India and not Australia will face England at Old Trafford. It will be a match of altogether less resonance and less difficulty for England.' The *Times* is echoing a similar sentiment: 'Full house should see England triumph, in spite of Kapil Dev.' The *Sun* has an article solely dedicated to Roger Binny. 'Ah, at least someone's talking us up,' reckons Srikkanth. 'Not quite,'

Man Singh is quick to burst the bubble. Turns out that the British press has dug out his family tree. 'The great-grandson of a Scotsman' is how they've described him. He's one of their own now, after his Man of the Match performance against Australia. Unusually, they've even dedicated extra print space to an Indian player by spelling out Binny's name in full: Roger Michael Humphrey Binny.

The manager can sense the mood change. From informal to intense. From irresolute to determined. He can now afford a quiet smile to himself, knowing he has hit the bull's eye. The captain wants to speak next.

'Yes, we never beat England in one day in England. But there is always first time,' he begins, as a loud cheer follows.

'Cheeka, you have to hit.'

'Jimmy pa, you stay.'

'Yash, you play without fear.'

Meanwhile, Kirti, as he often does, has sneaked up behind Kapil, miming a catch at every grammatical error his skipper makes.

'Sandy, you become a lion,' Kapil carries on, unperturbed.

'Kiri, you catch every ball.'

'And last one, Sunny paaji, it is high time you get runs,' he ends his speech nonchalantly, breaking into a smile. But he's the only one beaming. The mirth in the room has abruptly disappeared. Everyone, except Kapil, is looking at Gavaskar from the corner of their eyes. The master is glowering back. For the next few seconds, time stands still. The meeting is over. Everyone is back in their rooms.

Minutes later, Kapil knocks on Sandeep's door.

'What's it, Kaps?' asks Sandeep, standing at the door, wearing a white polka-dotted shirt with a dagger collar, smelling of a strong eau de cologne.

'Have you seen my English cassette?' asks Kapil, suspecting that the quintessential prankster must have been at work.

'Kaps, my English is already bad, and I don't want to ruin it further by listening to your English cassette.'

Kapil can't help but laugh.

'Anyway, where are you off to?' the skipper wants to know, as he scans Sandeep, head to toe – from his shirt to his bell-bottoms, down to his high-heel shoes.

'We are heading out for a party,' Kirti interjects, as he walks into the conversation in the hotel corridor, dressed as niftily as his fellow partygoer tonight.

'Guys, you know I've never stopped anyone from doing anything so long as they give their 100 per cent on the field. You people have so much talent; use it fully by resting well ahead of a big game.'

'Skipper!' yells Sunil Valson from three doors away. 'Do you know that besides you, the vice captain and the manager, I am the only one in the team that has a room to himself?'

'What do you mean?'

'Because Kirti, my room partner, is out most nights,' says Valson, grinning, as Sandeep and Kirti disappear at the end of the corridor and into the elevator.

Listening to Kapil and Valson talk, Man Singh emerges from his room on the same floor, and gestures Kapil to come to him.

'What was that order to Sunny all about?' the soft-spoken manager wants to know inside the private confines of his room.

'I am the captain. Can't I ask questions of my team? Don't I have the right to speak my mind?' says Kapil in Hindi, confidently.

'Yes, Kapil, you do, but –'

'But?' Kapil can't stop himself from interjecting. He has plenty to say. 'Sunny too was my skipper not so long ago. He had once proclaimed that I'll never make a test half-century in my career.'

'So, is this what it's all about? Tit for tat?'

'No... Not at all.' Kapil knits his brow thoughtfully. 'I thought he had all the right to say that to me. In fact, his chiding, or anyone else's criticism, has always motivated me to do better. Why take things personally?'

'I understand your intentions, but it may have come across as if you were deriding him. I could see that Sunny wasn't too happy.'

'You know my English. Unlike you guys who come from a cultured background, mine is an agricultural background. But I don't regret saying what I said. Yes, it could have been said with a bit more grace, which I clearly lack.'

With that, Kapil walks out of the manager's suite. As he is about to open the door of his room, he spots two members of his team down the corridor entering their respective rooms. Kirti Azad and Sandeep Patil have decided to call it an early night. They have a World Cup semi-final to play tomorrow.

17

One-Day Mataram

22 June 1983, Manchester

Kapil's Devils have reached the ground early. The crowds are pouring in. The support, ostensibly, is overwhelmingly in favour of the hosts. It's been less than two weeks since the Conservatives, led by Margaret Thatcher, have been voted back into power by a thumping majority. British nationalism is at an all-time high.

Rajdeep is feeling low. It's a weekday, which means no club game for him, and a perfect opportunity to travel to Manchester and watch India play. But, try as much as he did, there isn't a ticket available. Instead, his day's plan includes mowing a couple of gardens in his neighbourhood to earn some much-needed pocket money. That'll make his life in England less difficult. The stipend he gets from playing cricket for a local club is never enough.

The Indian team is warming up. Sandeep Patil and Ravi Shastri have walked over to take a look at the strip on offer today. They like what they see. The 22 yards at Old Trafford is reminiscent of Green Park in Kanpur or Feroz Shah Kotla in New Delhi. They have a conversation – wordless, through the language of their eyes. The pitch looks slow and low, just the type our bowlers will relish, both agree. They walk back to the dressing room carrying a smug look on their faces.

Sunny's face looks sullen. The remarks made the previous evening are still occupying his mind. Man Singh sits him down.

'Sunny, listen –'

'You are free to leave me out of the playing XI if anyone has doubts over my commitment,' Gavaskar is quick to interject.

Having spoken his mind, he feels 10 kilos lighter. But the prospect of two of the biggest stars in his team at loggerheads is weighing heavily on the rotund manager's mind.

'Not at all! Please don't think like that. You know English isn't Kapil's strongest suit. I am sure he didn't mean what he said,' says Man Singh by way of an explanation to the most senior member of the team.

With an important match about to begin, the former captain allows the matter to rest.

'Heads,' calls Kapil, as Bob Willis flicks the coin in the air. Tails it is. England are batting. Not surprising given the dry nature of the pitch. And with the sun beating down on this unusually hot day, it's only going to get tougher to bat in the second half.

Things are heating up in the stands too. A couple of English supporters have been ejected from the ground by the stewards for racial taunts. They weren't sitting too far from Harry Bhatia and his mates, in the section of the ground dominated by local fans. At the other end, Bhatia senior and his friends have found an easier way to deal with the heat: chilled lagers in hand at 10 in the morning. Behind them, stands an Indian fan with a banner supported by wooden sticks at both ends. It is large enough for it to be spotted by the BBC cameras spread across the ground. It reads: Dev-astation.

Ayaz has walked up a floor and settled down in his chair at the press box. 'After Tunbridge Wells, could this be another historic day for Indian cricket?' he wonders, before allowing his reverie to go one step further. 'What if Pakistan were to beat the West Indies in the other semi-final? Imagine a final between India and Pakistan!' His flight of fantasy is brought to an abrupt halt by a conversation taking place right next to him. Two journalists are exchanging notes about India's prospects today. One of them mentions the bookmakers' odds for the day – 50:1 for an India win.

'If that happens, it will be the biggest upset on English soil since a filly named Foinavon won the Grand National at the odds of 100:1, 16 years ago,' reminds the other. That other is David Frith. Editor of the *Wisden Cricket Monthly*. The predictor of India's impending failure at the World Cup, at the start of the tournament. This is the first India game he is covering in the World Cup. And it's not his fault. It's the first game the Indians are playing that's worth his while. Ayaz has both heard and read of Mr Frith's work. Good opportunity for an apprentice to pick the veteran's brains? Not quite. The senior pro isn't indulging the rookie. Not really forthcoming with tips. Not sure if these Indian scribes know anything about a quintessentially English sport.

Graeme Fowler is walking the talk. Playing with the same confidence he displayed in the BBC studios last night. A flick off Balwinder Singh Sandhu to square leg to bring up the first boundary of the day. The crowd roars. The decibel levels suggest a large majority in the grounds is backing the home team.

At the end of 7 overs, England are 20 for no loss. Even singles are being cheered with much gusto. Bright sunshine, bare chests, white floppy hats all around. Now it's Chris Tavaré's turn to hit a 4 off Sandhu. Legendary for his slow scoring – as one scribe put it, for Tavaré, making runs was 'a disagreeable, even vulgar, distraction from the pure task of surviving' – his well-timed square cut has brought up England's 50 in the 12th over.

The word has gone out. More people are filtering into the stadium, lack of space notwithstanding. The organizers may have oversold tickets. White iron railings, built to separate one stand from another, are being used as ad hoc seats.

The scorers stationed inside the giant black scoreboard are being kept busy – the bald, bespectacled man in charge of moving the runs column busier than the tall, bearded man responsible for changing the wicket number. England are 69 for no loss in 16 overs. Plenty of English flags, sporting the traditional red cross against the white backdrop, are being enthusiastically waved across the stands. The Indian bowlers need some nursing.

Roger Binny is brought into the attack. He attacks Tavaré outside the off stump. The outswinger narrowly misses the outside edge. Another one on the off stump, this one holds its line after pitching, kisses the edge of the bat and lands safely inside Syed Kirmani's gloves.

Before Tavaré can find a chair to sit in the dressing room, his opening partner, Fowler, follows him there. It is Binny again. Bowling over the wicket, despite a left-hander being on strike, he gets the ball to land in line with the middle stump, and then, move it away to hit the off stump. The great-grandson of a Scotsman has won over the great-grandson of an Englishman. 84 for two in 20.3 overs.

In the shop, at the corner of Baker Street in London, Pooja Parekh switches on the radio placed behind the cash counter. Turns the volume up, a few notches above normal.

Loud enough for her father to hear the match commentary in the storeroom at the back of the shop, where he's busy arranging the fresh stock that has just arrived. Listening to the live commentary of the wickets that have just fallen, Jiten Bhai walks over to the counter. Turns off the radio. Pooja understands. He has probably not forgiven himself for placing a 600-pound bet on cricket, and letting his wife and the whole family down.

The 100 is up for England in the 25th over, with Allan Lamb running 2 off Binny. At the other end, David Gower is missing more often than connecting. The elegant left-hander is not looking his usual self.

Jimmy Amarnath is not bowling his usual stuff. The outswinger, his stock delivery in the tournament, has not been working. So, he's switched to inswingers. Gower is his first casualty. The inswinger becomes an outswinger for the left-hander, and has found the outside edge of the bat and settled inside Kirmani's gloves.

Kirti Azad is brought into the attack. He's the only spin-bowling all-rounder in the playing XI. His off spin has been preferred ahead of Ravi Shastri's left-arm orthodox, considering the number of left-handers in England's squad. For the right-handers, Kirti has adopted a leg-stump line, stifling them in the process. 'Negative' is how one radio commentator describes it. A collective 'boo' is the crowd's reaction. Jimmy and Kirti, bowling in tandem, have bowled 6 overs apiece. England's scoring rate has come down drastically. After 35 overs, the hosts find themselves on 127 for 3. It's been 11 overs without a boundary.

Umpire David Evans has called lunch. Kirti, the reserve bowler of the day, gets a pat from his captain as they walk off the ground. The off-spinner, having bowled 6 overs already, reckons he's done for the day. 'Do you need me to bowl after lunch or should I change my bowling boots (spikes) and wear the (more comfortable) ripples?' 'Whatever you feel like,' says the skipper.

First over after lunch, Kapil throws the ball to Kirti. The bowler, not wearing his bowling spikes, knits his brow in confusion before giving his cap to the umpire. The first ball is a poor one: down the leg-side. Mike Gatting bends down on his knees and gives it the treatment it deserves. 4 down to fine leg. The perils of adopting a leg-stump line. Dead accurate, you can stifle runs; slightly wayward, it turns into a gift for the batsman. Yashpal at short-fine leg has no chance of stopping it. 'Push the fine leg back,' screams restaurateur-turned-cricket expert Mintu Bhatia from the stands. Kapil can't hear him, or is choosing not to. Either way, Yashpal is staying put inside the 30-yard circle.

Same over, similar ball, Allan Lamb tries a similar shot. Only this time, the short-fine leg fielder stops the ball in its path, picks it up, and hits the stumps at the non-striker's end. All in one motion. Allan Lamb is run-out. The badam-fed strong hands of Yashpal Sharma to the fore.

Rajdeep has allowed his arms and the lawnmower some rest. He is sitting on the front lawn of a row house, under a tree, a glass of lemonade in hand, alongside the owner of the property, listening to live commentary from Manchester on a portable radio. As he takes a sip of the ice-cold beverage, he can't help but admire the freshly manicured grass and India's performance so far, in equal measure.

Amarnath seems to have got a measure of Gatting. Bowling from the Warwick Road end, he releases yet another inswinger. The ball nips back sharply and disturbs Gatting's stumps. The scoreboard reads 150 for 5 in 42 overs. The 'Dev-astation' banner, which was quietly, and quickly, placed in hiding, is out again, floating in the mild summer breeze.

But things are about to get hot. Ian Botham has walked in. For a battle within a war. The one everyone has been waiting for. The clash of two of the best all-rounders in the world. Kapil versus Botham. Before Kapil though, Kirti is allowed to have a go at the man, who single-handedly won the Ashes two years ago. Kapil, expecting a couple of lusty blows, pushes three fielders to the leg-side boundary. There are six in all on the on-side, leaving the off-side largely exposed. Botham looks around the field and takes strike. His mind is busy calculating what he has got to do. Reverse sweep – a shot rarely seen – is executed to perfection. The crowd lets out a collective 'wow!' in response to the sheer audacity of the shot. Kirti reassesses the situation. His mind is made up. The leg-stump line and the heavy deployment of fielders on the on-side must stay. The next ball follows the same trajectory, but marginally slower than the one before. Botham is committed to exploiting the gaps on the off-side. He takes a step back and makes space. He's gauged the line and length. The idea is to play against the spin. Botham takes a big swipe at the ball. Commanding his willow to come down on the ball. All's under control. Wood hits ball! Or has ball hit wood? The bails are on the floor. Nothing could have prepared Botham for what has just happened. The red leather cherry refused to rise after pitching. Running along the surface, much like a bowling ball striking 10 pins, or three in this case. Any lower and it would have gone underground. Botham has encountered nothing like this in his seven years of international cricket; his reaction says it all – slamming the bat on the ground, he walks off in frustration.

David Frith is shaking his head. There is some mention of 1981, Trevor Chappell and Brian McKechnie in the press box. Ostensibly in jest. 'This came from over the arm, gentlemen,' Ayaz mutters, before enjoying a quiet snigger.

Srikkanth jumps over, squealing a 'well bowled, da' in Kirti's ears, while hanging like a rucksack on his back, as the rest of the team forms a huddle around them. A bunch of people from the crowd have also made their way to the centre. The team huddle can't stop them from stuffing currency notes in Kirti's pocket. It ranges from one-pound coins to 20-pound notes.

The 75-yard walk, followed by a flight of stairs to the dressing room, hasn't been of much help in bringing Botham's temperature down. He swings his bat wildly in the air just as he enters the dressing room. The bat catches air, followed by a pot of tea. The hot, aromatic beverage quickly spreads across the floor. Trouble is brewing for the fancied hosts.

'Well bowled, Kirti! But tell me, the ball usually stays low or turns. How did this stay low and turn?' a happy, yet bewildered Kapil wants to know, arm around Kirti's shoulder. 'This is my trade secret; I put my index finger under the seam to make the ball squat. I've specially learnt how to bowl this delivery,' says Kirti in all seriousness, even as he's chuckling inside.

Kirti has given his earnings to the umpire for safe-keeping. Coins of all denominations. The janitor in the English dressing room has earned his daily wage too. The floor is gleaming once again. England reeling at 160 for 6 in 46 overs.

A few tip-and-runs and inside edges push the score past 200. Kapil is to bowl the last over. He's gunning for extra pace. One has gone for 4 off the edge. Another has reached the boundary, missing the batsman and the keeper. Ultra-wide. Kapil is livid with himself. The senior pro Gavaskar walks up to his skipper. Pats his waist with both hands and asks him to 'buck up'. Kapil picks up a wicket off the last ball of the innings. His opposite number, Bob Willis, is bowled. England 213 all out, in 60 overs.

Walking off the field, Kirti reckons it's now a good time to ask his skipper what he's been meaning to ask for some time now. 'You should have told me if you wanted me to bowl after lunch. I wouldn't have changed my shoes.' The instinctive captain that Kapil is, smiles. 'If I had, you would have started thinking extra about how to bowl the next 6 overs; so I thought best not to tell you so that you don't overthink.'

Mintu and friends haven't had to think too hard about what to grab for lunch. They've headed straight for the only truck serving Indian food at the stadium today. Chicken tikka masala on their mind. 'Sorry, we are out of it,' says the lady at the counter. The demand exceeding the supply by a large margin. Vegetable samosas are all that's left. Not quite what Mintu's Punjabi palate desires today. Especially not after all those beers. So, fish and chips will have to do. They join the queue. After a 10-minute wait, it's finally their turn. Three roughnecks barge in, jumping the queue. Mintu objects. 'Go back to where you came from,' he's told. Saran and Kulwant rein in their friend. Mintu swallows his pride.

Harry is standing just metres away, watching the transgression up close. Yet, he chooses not to intervene. The boys are his friends, bringing him his lunch, as he fetches more beers for the gang.

The English team is unhappy with 213. Yashpal is unhappier still. Someone has polished off the almonds from his plate. He brought them with him from the hotel, for refreshment during the innings break, since there wouldn't be much on offer at the ground for a vegetarian like him.

Sandeep Patil, due to bat at no. 5, is busy playing tennis-ball cricket in the dressing room. Balwinder Singh Sandhu giving him company. Now they stop. Gavaskar is beginning to put on his pads – always the left one first. No one dares make any noise. The master's getting into his zone. His opening partner isn't around. Srikkanth is on the balcony, smoking. He was in the changing room a short while back, pacing up and down, wearing his pads, holding his bat, twirling it around, hitting someone while swinging it, slapping someone on the back, stepping on someone's shoes – generally creating havoc. Now, a few puffs of tobacco later, he seems in control of all the nervous energy in his body. He's talking to Binny, casually, cigarette in mouth, à la Clint Eastwood. The Chennai resident picked up smoking during his engineering years to deal with the immense pressure of exams. Legend has it that a selector once gave him a choice:

leave smoking or risk never being selected. 'Take a walk,' is how he's supposed to have responded.

The Indian openers have responded well to begin with. It is a cautious, yet solid start. All part of a plan of playing out the opening spell of Willis and Botham without losing a wicket. Gavaskar and Srikkanth are following it to a T. India can't afford to lose early wickets, lest the middle order comes under pressure. It is 21 for no loss, after 10 overs.

Local boy Paul Allott is handed the ball. He runs in full steam and lets it rip. The ball meets the full face of Gavaskar's bat. With the Duncan Fearnley sticker on it, looking straight into the bowler's eye. The ball is dispatched to the long-off boundary. Gavaskar stands still, balanced. Left elbow high. The arm guard – suspended in the air, vertically – watching over the ball travelling to the boundary. For the first time in this tournament, the Little Master, seemingly, is in the mood.

Srikkanth doesn't need any excuse to be in the mood. He bludgeons one over Bob Willis, at mid-off, for 4. Botham, the bowler, hands on his hips, isn't too pleased.

The pleasing-to-the-eye Gavaskar is out. Against the run of play. 'It's a wicket England badly wanted,' is the TV commentator's opinion.

Srikkanth isn't done with Botham yet. The stroke maker pulls a short one to the square-leg fence. 'Get that line straight,' is skipper Willis's advice to the bowler.

Jimmy Amarnath, wearing his lucky shirt, washed fresh after every match, and carrying his lucky red handkerchief in his pocket, has joined Srikkanth in the middle.

It's third time lucky for Botham. This one has ballooned up. Srikkanth's natural instincts getting the better of him. He has swung his bat fractionally early, allowing the ball to hit it a bit higher than intended. Willis is taking no chances. 'It's mine,' he screams, running from mid-off and completing the catch at mid-on. Srikkanth is walking back to the pavilion, dragging his Slazenger bat along the turf. Visibly disappointed. India are two down for 50.

Make that three down. Mike Gatting has knocked the stumps down at the non-striker's end with Yashpal Sharma inches short. It's the batsman's fault, attempting a suicidal run after the ball has gone straight into the hands of the mid-on fielder. But Yashpal is still in the middle. It's the umpire's fault. David Evans has failed to spot the run-out, despite being in the perfect position to do so. The English players are perplexed, the fans vexed.

Amarnath and Yashpal have taken a conscious call to be cautious. Extra cautious. 'No wicket should fall now; doesn't matter if we don't get runs,' is Amarnath's standing instruction. 'Okay, Jimmy pa,' answers Yashpal in the affirmative. The next 12 overs bring 14 runs. No wickets.

The tension in the Indian dressing room is palpable. Kirti, Patil and Kapil are sitting on the balcony. Pads on legs, hands in gloves trepidation writ large on their faces. Gavaskar is sitting a few steps behind. Kapil can't sit still any longer; he gets up and starts pacing around the dressing room. 'Who do you think should go next?' Kapil wants Gavaskar's help. 'Don't panic, all three of you have the ability to up the tempo. Whoever goes, will score.' Kapil sits back down on his chair.

Fans in India, cheering and on their feet just a short while ago, have also sat down, deflated. Unable to comprehend the live images on their black-and-white TV screens. 'What is going on? Why aren't they scoring?' are the questions they are asking one another, with no one to answer them. Those watching the same pictures on their colour TVs in England have better access. The telephone in the pavilion of the Old Trafford Cricket Ground in Manchester is inundated with calls from across the UK. Man Singh has to answer all of them. One of them happens to be from the manager's brother-in-law. 'What's happening? We'll lose the match at this rate!' He's echoing exactly what every other caller had to say. 'This is all part of a plan, they know what they are doing,' is Man Singh's standard response, without having a clue himself what the men in the middle plan to do.

Allott to Amarnath. He executes a classic square cut. The ball runs down for a 4. It's a rare boundary. India's 100 comes up in the 34th over. The last 20 overs have accounted for 50 runs. Tea is called.

Yashpal and Amarnath walk into a dead-silent dressing room. The usual chatter is missing. There are no customary pats on the backs from their teammates. No one has bothered to offer them tea either. The not-out batsmen can sense the tension in the air. Spotting Man Singh sitting in a corner, sipping tea, Amarnath gesticulates to him to come over. 'Is our scoring rate the cause of worry?' he asks, softly. The manager responds with a set smile on his face. Amarnath has his answer. He reciprocates with a broad smile of his own. 'Don't worry, we know what we are doing; just stay calm and relax,' says Amarnath, before taking the last sip from his tea cup, wearing his gloves, and heading back on to the field. The 44-year-old cricket administrator can instantly feel an abatement in his anxiety levels, leading to an increase in his appetite levels. Another cup of tea and an extra piece of cake are had.

True to his words, the first over after lunch, Amarnath steps down the track. And collects a 4. 'There is no point in both of us taking a risk. I'll go after the bowling, you stay put,' are the vice captain's instructions when the two batsmen meet in the centre of the pitch for a chat. 'Yes, of course, Jimmy pa,' says Yashpal.

'Let's have faith in them, guys. If these two stay till the end, we will win,' the experienced Gavaskar has a word of advice for the tense Indian camp.

A couple of steps down the pitch. Leaving the stumps exposed, daring the bowler to hit them. A flat-batted swipe.

Off Paul Allott. The ball sailing over the long-off fence. It's a 6. It's not Amarnath. It's Yashpal. Hitting the ball with disdain. The vice captain is taken aback. 'Listen to me, Yash, just chill a bit; we don't want to lose a wicket.' The hot-blooded Punjabi nods in agreement.

Skipper Bob Willis comes into the attack. Yashpal has been shuffling across his stumps repeatedly. The bowler has spotted the pronounced movement at the crease. He's now trying to bowl a middle-stump line. Inswingers at that. The idea is to have the batsman dismissed LBW. Yashpal grins. The line has been cast. He's been working on it for the last four years. Trying it out in the nets. And today, Willis has fallen for it, hook, line and sinker.

Next ball. Willis, running in. Yashpal has his eyes fixed on him. But his mind is elsewhere. 1979 to be precise. The West Indies versus England in a World Cup final. Viv Richards moves across his stumps, picks up Mike Hendricks's delivery from outside the off-stump, and sends it across to the square-leg boundary for a maximum. Yashpal, sitting in the stands, watches the ball drop – along with his jaw – right in front of him.

The cheer from the crowd has brought him back to his senses. He looks around. The ball is being retrieved from the deep square-leg boundary. The umpire has both his arms up in the air. Bob Willis stands 10 yards in front of him. Yashpal is standing at one end of the batting strip. The off-stump right behind him. The scorer is adding 6 runs to Yashpal's individual score. 'Sublime shot!' yells the commentator. He doesn't know it was subliminal.

Amarnath doesn't know what to make of it. He enjoyed the audacious shot, but isn't too pleased with Yashpal's cavalier approach. 'Good shot, yaar; but why are you batting so aggressively, almost angrily?' the senior pro wants to know. 'Jimmy pa, you don't know, he swore at me in Madras. I have been waiting for an opportunity to give it back!'

Eighteen months ago: Yashpal Sharma reaches a plucky half-century on day two of the Madras test between India and England. Rather than appreciate his batting, Ian Botham and Bob Willis use profanity to describe the landmark. The temperamental Yashpal is seething. He is on the verge of using his bat for something other than just smacking balls. His partner at the other end, the ice-cool Gundappa Viswanath, comes to the rescue with his pearls of wisdom. 'Just score a 100 and then not you, but the English media will sledge them back, you watch.' Yashpal obliges, brings up his second test century, before the end of the day's play. The crowds applaud. The opposition ignores.

The largely ignored Indians in England are feeling boisterous today. They sense a major upset in the cards. '*Angrezon ko sabak sikhana hai* – We have to teach the English a lesson' chants can be heard emanating from the stands, drowning the chorus of an improvised version of 'God Save the Queen' – featuring words like 'no surrender', borrowed from a xenophobic song of the same name – being sung by the English supporters. Yashpal and Amarnath are marching on.

Rajdeep has returned home after a long day of working in the neighbourhood lawns. The match is playing on TV. He settles down on the couch, next to his landlady. Mrs Symonds is an avid cricket fan herself. Having spent many a summer watching the gentleman's game. 'This is history in the making,' she tells Rajdeep. The 18-year-old student, still unsure about the result, however, has no reason to doubt his host's prophecy. She speaks from experience, he knows well.

A gentle sweep off off-spinner Vic Marks sees Yashpal bring up a well-deserved half-century. He has lost his partner Amarnath in the process – run-out for 46. Sandeep Patil joins him in the middle. 'You please stay till the end, I will take the risks,' is what the dashing stroke maker from Bombay tells Yashpal.

Bob Willis comes running in with the ball from close to the sight screen. Now the ball is running back towards the sight screen, following the exact same path, for a boundary. Sandeep Patil looks in the mood. Similar to what he was in exactly a year ago, on this very ground, against the very same bowler: Six consecutive 4s in a seven-ball over was what Willis was subjected to by Patil on that occasion.

It's Allott's turn now. A quick, short ball is nonchalantly dispatched to the square-leg boundary. Courtesy a textbook pull. But not all shots from Patil this afternoon are following the coaching manuals. Some are being labelled 'outlandish'. India's 200 is up on the scoreboard. Patil on 36, at the end of the 52nd over.

Man Singh, in his blue shirt and tie, is enjoying the action sitting in the player's balcony. Syed Kirmani is next to him, chewing his nails out of habit, not nervousness. Kapil is standing by with his pads on. 'India are sailing home,' is the latest pronouncement from the commentators.

Kapil is now walking out to bat. Yashpal is walking off to a standing ovation. Out for 61. Allott taking a stunning catch at the third-man boundary. Too little too late for England, perhaps? Kapil certainly thinks so. Standing at the non-striker's end, his broad smile is a dead giveaway. Just nine more runs needed. The Indian skipper can now envision 25 June, Lord's.

Good lord! There is a pitch invasion. Patil's drive to extra cover has fetched India just 2 runs. There's still a run needed to win. The incursion was premature. The invaders are trying to grab hold of the stumps. Umpire Don Oslear has pulled a wicket out. Raising it in his hand, threatening to hit anyone that dare come near him. Cops and ground stewards have run in to the rescue. The field is finally cleared. Play is ready to recommence.

The entire field stands on the off-side. Closer to the pavilion. All in readiness to run as soon as the winning runs are hit. Patil can't help but smile at the field placement. Willis comes running in. The ball is running to third man. The players are running to the pavilion. The rampaging fans are running to the field. A train is running in the background. India are the runaway winners.

Fights break out between the two sets of supporters. 'Kapil eats Botham for breakfast', reads a banner in the stands.

Dinner is served at the Symonds household in Worthing, West Essex. 'You must go watch your team play the World Cup finals. It's a once-in-a-lifetime opportunity,' is Mrs Symonds advice to her paying guest. Rajdeep's mind is made up. He isn't going to miss it for the world.

In news coming in, Pakistan have been pummelled by the mighty West Indies in the other semi-final in London. No dream final then, between arch-rivals India and Pakistan, as some had hoped for. Reports suggest that captain Imran Khan wasn't fit enough to bowl and Javed Miandad wasn't well enough to play.

Kapil feels vindicated. As is evident from his post-match statement in the press room. 'We had personal score to settle. English players, press and people did not think we were worthy of reaching the finals. Me and my boys wanted to prove them wrong.' His counterpart, Bob Willis, is gracious in defeat. 'India have been grossly underrated. I don't know why people always expect them to lose.' David Gower offers a more analytical reaction. 'The Indians have really learnt how to field in one-day cricket. But I believe it was their teamwork and Kapil's astute captaincy that won them the game.'

The press briefing is over. Ayaz Memon walks past David Frith and slips him the latest copy of the *Wisden Cricket Monthly*, pointing to an article on the second page. In the 'Letters to the Editor' section, a certain Man Singh from New Jersey in the USA has written a piece reminding Frith of his article published at the start of the tournament dismissing India altogether. And now that India has reached the knockouts, Singh wants the *Wisden* editor to retract his words. What's more, a mere verbal retraction wouldn't do for Singh – he suggests that Frith eat his words, literally.

Frith peers over his spectacles at Ayaz. Of course, he had read the letter before. As the editor, he had allowed it to be printed in the first place. He then smiles and shows him the thumbs up sign. He's game.

There is a huge presence of fans at the entrance of the Indian team hotel. Mostly young English kids with their scrapbooks that feature rare photographs of the Indian players. They are seeking autographs. The World Cup finalists oblige. Mintu Bhatia and friends are also at the hotel lobby. Unlike London, Mintu doesn't own a restaurant in Manchester. But he's got an Indian dinner organized. His close proximity to a few members of the Indian team has allowed him to extend an invitation to the entire squad.

The party is at an Indian restaurant in downtown Manchester. It's owned by a friend of Mintu's, Tanwir Mohammad, a businessman of Pakistani origin. The champagne is chilling on ice. The celebrations run late into the night. No worries. There are no early-morning engagements tomorrow. No match. No practice. The team is scheduled to leave for London only after lunch.

Two brown-skinned boys walk into Jiten Bhai's shop. The shop owner is busy doing his accounts. His daughter is cleaning the floor. 'Could we get a couple of beers, please?' asks one of them politely. 'No, we are closed,' says Jiten Bhai, without even bothering to look up. 'Come on, sir, can't you make an exception tonight? At least as a fellow Indian. We are celebrating. It's not often that we play the final of a World Cup.' The man at the cash counter now looks up. After a brief pause, he puts his book of accounts aside. Then, gestures towards Pooja with a partial shake of his head. Pooja hands them two cans of beer. The boys run out, leaving the cash on the counter, saying a loud 'thank you!' Jiten Bhai puts the money in the cash drawer. He allows himself a half-smile. Pooja sees this from the corner of her eye. The daughter can't help but flash a beaming smile.

18

Act One
The Pledge

23 June 1983

Mintu is at the wheel, cruising down the M6 from Manchester to London in his Mercedes. The seat next to him is empty. On it lies this morning's edition of the *Sun* – the most-read tabloid in England. The front-page headline states: SHAME ON ENGLAND! On the back seat lies Harry. His left eye swollen. Caught in the crossfire of the brawl that broke out after the game last evening. The natives mistook him for an immigrant Indian. Can't blame them entirely. They would never have known that underneath the brown exterior resides the heart of an Englishman. Kulwant is sitting in his regular spot, right behind Mintu. The third musketeer, Saran, is further back, driving the indisposed Harry's red convertible back home.

24 June 1983, London

The Indian team is at Lord's Cricket Ground. Less than 24 hours to go for the biggest game of their lives. Kapil peeps at the 22 yards in the centre of the ground, while walking towards the practice pitches at the Nursery end – the eastern-most part of the ground.

At practice, Sandhu is picking Madan Lal's brains. 'Paaji, how do you bowl the off-cutter at will?' Madan takes the ball from Sandhu and demonstrates it to him: 'Just hold the ball like this, and throw it like this.' 'Like what?' asks Sandhu, scratching his patka. 'Oh, like this.' Madan executes the action again. Sandhu walks away, disappointed. He's thinking Madan paaji doesn't want to share his trade secret with him. The truth is, Madan paaji can't articulate half as well as he can make the ball talk.

Nonetheless, Balwinder is determined to master the craft, as he sends down inswinger after inswinger in the nets. Captain Kapil isn't impressed. 'Oye, sardar, concentrate on outswing. Only outswingers get you wickets at the international level.' Sandhu nods.

Will it be a swing-friendly pitch? That's the topic of discussion as Kapil's Devils gather around for the pre-final team meeting. Kapil has been left astounded by the amount of grass he saw on the pitch a short while ago. He's convinced it will all be shaved off by the time they return to the ground tomorrow. 'They can't have such a green and bouncy track for a one-day game,' he tells his teammates.

Ravi Shastri isn't playing the final. Despite his stellar performances in both the recent one-day wins against the West Indies – at Berbice and Manchester. Kirti Azad has been preferred because of the crucial role he played in the semi-final win over England. Undeterred, Shastri is keeping himself busy. Man Singh has just revealed how much the team will win as prize money if they can upset the reigning World Champions tomorrow; and the inborn businessman in Shastri is already calculating how much each member of the team will get, breaking the 20,000-pound figure down to the decimal point.

In news coming in, Clive Lloyd has just announced that he will step down as captain of the West Indies soon after tomorrow's final. There's no doubt his teammates would like to give him a memorable farewell. What better than a hat-trick of world titles?

Rajdeep can't wait to witness history. He's sourced a ticket for the finals. Thanks to his father, Dilip Sardesai, a former test cricketer, who's flown in from India to witness the biggest game in cricket.

A few more like Sardesai Sr have made the journey to Old Blighty from India. But not all of them are as lucky as Rajdeep. Tickets for the final are as rare as a day of sunshine in England.

N.K.P. Salve, the current chief of Indian cricket, has put in a request with the Marylebone Cricket Club, or MCC, for two extra VIP passes for his friends, who have flown in from India especially for the game. After a brief discussion amongst its members, MCC, the governing body for the game in England and Wales, has informed Mr Salve that his request cannot be entertained. Worse still, even paid tickets aren't available, he's told. It's an unusual position for a board chief, Congress politician and Member of Parliament to find himself in. Repudiation isn't a common occurrence in his life in India. How to deal with this indignity, he knows not. But deal with it he must, he knows.

For now, the MCC must handle its own mess. The custodians of the laws of cricket find themselves in an embarrassing position of having made no provisions for match passes for the Indian pressmen covering the event. 'Didn't expect India to make it this far,' is the only explanation they have to offer. It's as weak a defence as Fowler's against Binny in the semi-final. After much supplication, followed by cogitation, the six Indian journalists are handed their press passes. Ayaz breathes a sigh of relief.

Mintu and friends aren't losing sleep. They have a plan in place. Paying a premium for a match ticket isn't a problem for them. Plus, there will be plenty of disappointed Englishmen willing to sell their tickets after their team failed to make it to the finals.

19

Act Two
The Turn

25 June 1983, London

The Indian team enters the hallowed turf of Lord's Cricket Ground for the very first time this tournament. They've been at the practice facilities a couple of times during this World Cup, but this is the first time they'll be playing here in this championship. The organizers are not to be blamed – Kapil and his men weren't a top-draw team to merit a game at the Home of Cricket. Now, they've forced their way through. And are warming up in a corner of the field.

The BBC crew stands a few metres away. Anchorman Peter West and former cricketers Richie Benaud, Fred Trueman and Jim Laker are setting up the game for their viewers. The topic of discussion is India's abysmal record at this very ground. So far, the Indian team has played 10 tests here and have failed to win even one. Two draws and eight defeats in all. This also includes the 1974 test that saw Ajit Wadekar's team being bowled out for 42, in just 77 minutes, against England. India's lowest-ever score in a test match. The seventh lowest in the 106-year-old history of test cricket.

The crowd is beginning to trickle in. After 30 minutes of analysis, the BBC men are taking a break. Madan Lal is walking back to the dressing room before the captains come out for the toss. Peter West gives him a shout-out, 'Hey, Madan, hope you guys win; it will be great for the game of cricket.' Madan, with a half-smile, nods. Unable to ignore the volte-face of the broadcasters. Just three days ago, they had got India knocked out of the tournament even before it could step out to play the semi-final. Today is a new day.

For once, Kapil's soothsaying powers have disappointed him. The pitch hasn't been worked upon overnight to make it more conducive for one-day cricket. The grass on the strip is as thick and green as it was yesterday. Win the toss and bowl, it's a no-brainer. And Clive Lloyd has done just that. Kapil is walking away disappointed. Lloyd isn't even trying to hide his grin.

However, skipper Kapil is doing a good job of not showing his discontent to his mates in the dressing room. 'We will never get another day like this. Forget about winning, just enjoy. At least we've reached this far,' is his message before the game.

The team too seems convinced. So are the BCCI president and secretary. President N.K.P. Salve and secretary M.A. Chidambaram reiterate what Kapil has just told his troupe. 'Just play the match without any pressure,' they say, before adding, 'Win or lose, the board will pay 25,000 rupees to each player.' The announcement has lit up a few pairs of eyes in an already wide-eyed team.

It's a pleasant Saturday afternoon. Not as hot as the days leading up to the final. The players are all wearing jumpers. The crowds have their jackets and cardigans on. There isn't an empty seat inside Lord's. In fact, many find themselves sitting on the ground, in the space between the stands and the boundary rope. Around 25,000 is the reported figure of spectators. Way above the official capacity of the stadium. The Indian team too has contributed to the overflow. Smuggling in a few fans and friends in their team bus.

Mintu, Saran and Kulwant bought their tickets this morning from right outside Lord's, just as they had planned. There are plenty of England fans selling theirs at a small premium. The Southall residents now find themselves in the middle of a curry party, with fellow Indian supporters playing the dholaks and striking temple bells to a disharmonious tune. Harry sits at home, nursing his bruised eye.

The West Indian fans outnumber their Indian counterparts. With their cymbals and bongos, they've turned this into a carnival even before the delivery of the first ball. Amongst them sits Rajdeep. Thankfully, he has found compatriot company. Two friends from Bombay. Jitu Parmar and Yajurvindra Singh are first-class cricketers, who are playing the role of coach and manager respectively for a school team from Rajkot that has come to England to play cricket as part of an exchange programme. The three of them are wedged between the stylish Caribbean folk wearing wide-collar shirts, bell-bottoms and leather caps. They've come to see their team lift the World Cup three times in a row. Rajdeep and Co. are just happy to make up the numbers.

Ayaz is missing in action. Stuck in the infamous London traffic. He had the option of taking the underground. But that would have meant changing two trains to reach Lord's from Surbiton, where he's staying. His friend and host, Imtiaz, suggested he take a cab instead. 'Bad advice,' Ayaz is thinking, sitting at the back of a London black cab, '40 pounds for reaching late and watching India lose, what a waste!'

Srikkanth and Gavaskar have walked out to bat after a last-minute piece of advice from Kapil: 'The pitch is 70 per cent for bowlers and 30 per cent for batsmen, so be careful against their fast bowlers. Just wait for the part-time spin of Richards and Gomes to score off.' Gavaskar is doing just that. Taking his time to settle in. Srikkanth is humming his favourite Bollywood song, *'Tere mere beech mein kaisa hai yeh bandhan* – Oh, what's this bond between us', both while batting and while standing at the non-striker's end, ensuring he and his partner are stress-free in the middle of a high-stakes encounter.

Ayaz has finally reached. And is rushing towards the Grace Gates, named after a legend of the sport, W.G. Grace. Just passing through this iconic iron-made erection is no less than a pilgrimage for this cricket romantic. Even the stiff upper-lipped stewards manning the entrance seem a bit distracted today, still unable to process India's successful run in the tournament. 'Oh, so we now have Gandhi coming to Lord's,' Ayaz hears one of them remark, an obvious reference to the Hollywood film of the same name that bagged eight Academy awards just a couple of months ago. Just as Ayaz is walking up the stairs, towards the press box, a loud cheer erupts. He can't see the live action yet, but can hear the distinct Caribbean beat from the stands. He fears the worst. A former Australian captain, now commentator, Richie Benaud is walking down. 'What do you say, I'll still offer you 66:1 odds for an India win today. Want to wager?' he asks Ayaz. 'No, thanks, Richie. I've just wasted 40 pounds on a cab. Don't want to waste 10 more.'

Sitting in the press box, right above the square-leg fielder, Ayaz's fear has come true. With grey hair protruding from behind his ears, Sunil Gavaskar is walking back after scoring just 2. Caught by wicketkeeper Jeff Dujon off an Andy Roberts outswinger.

On a green and damp pitch, Andy Roberts and Joel Garner are showcasing the full range of their armoury. Garner, all of 6 feet, 8 inches, is getting the ball to rise menacingly. Roberts is bowling flat and fast. Survival is tough.

Now, here's one that pitches on a good length, and Srikkanth puts his front leg forward, bat alongside, in a bid to offer a textbook front-foot defence to a Garner delivery. But the ball nips back sharply after pitching, rises more than expected, and hits him on his gloves.

'The skipper's advice be damned, it's time for Plan B,' Srikkanth tells himself. Andy Roberts bowls a short one. The opener rocks back, swings his bat horizontally and pulls the ball from outside the off stump, sending it to the midwicket boundary for 4.

Next up, Roberts bowls an even shorter one. A bit quicker this time. Srikkanth's bat swing is quicker too. The engineer-turned-cricketer has thrown caution to the winds. The ball is sailing over the square-leg boundary. 6! The 10-year-old Sachin Tendulkar, watching this on a black-and-white TV at a neighbour's house in Bombay, jumps up in excitement. So do his friends in the room. As have plenty of others in the stadium. Including Gundappa Viswanath. The accomplished batsman is sitting with his mates in the Indian dressing room.

Viswanath is one of Srikkanth's heroes. The apprentice is keen to impress the master. Andy Roberts will have to bear the brunt.

Srikkanth, Slazenger bat in hand, with its trademark 'V' on its face, now drops down on one knee, channelizes his inner Viswanath, and connects. The overpitched ball meets the meat of the bat and thuds into the signboard under the Tavern stand. Rattling it. The batsman holds his pose: bat held high – the black panther sticker on its back – right knee on the pitch, the top two buttons of his white shirt open, eyes following the trajectory of the ball, and 14 other men on the field standing motionless. Srikkanth has just played the shot of the tournament. Audacious and artistic in equal measure.

The best set of fast bowlers ever assembled under the sun is a bit taken aback. They aren't too familiar with Kris Srikkanth and his swashbuckling ways. They've only encountered the 23-year-old twice before. That too, in this very tournament. And a total of 26 balls before this game is hardly enough time to gauge the ways and means of a batsman. In his 40-ball stay today, he's already used the cut, pull, drive and the hook.

Mohinder 'Jimmy' Amarnath, they are more familiar with. And it's no surprise that he is being peppered with a few short ones. But the battle-hardened veteran has been in the form of his life the past few months. His reputation of standing up to fast bowlers growing by the day.

After a lengthy spell, Garner and Roberts are rested. But that doesn't mark the end of the West Indian onslaught. Michael Holding and Malcolm Marshall are running in full steam.

The fiery Marshall sends down a quick bouncer. It's heading in the same direction as it did a few weeks ago – straight towards Amarnath's lips. His upper lip is now covered by a handlebar moustache, concealing the remains of the six stitches he received during the Barbados test. This time, however, before reaching his skin, the ball meets wood. It's heading towards the midwicket boundary. Amarnath, left leg in the air, has executed his trademark pull. Amarnath's Nataraja act! Three more runs – India 58 for 1 in the 19th over.

A run later, Srikkanth is out. Hit on his leg. Plumb in front of the stumps. Attempting a cross-batted swat to a Marshall in-cutter. A nothing shot after *the* shot. It was Marshall's last ball of his first spell of 6 overs. Srikkanth knew it. It's evident from his crawl back to the pavilion. The scoreboard blandly says 38 runs off 57 balls. It doesn't have the means to measure the impact or the bravado of the innings.

Yashpal pushes Michael Holding gently to covers, Amarnath wallops Larry Gomes through extra cover: two different approaches, with the same result, 4s. It's 90 for 2 at the halfway mark of the Indian innings. All is well with the world.

Jiten Bhai sits alone in his shop. Business is slow. Pooja has requested that she be allowed to come in late today – after her music recital at a community event in their neighbourhood. The radio sits at its usual spot, behind the cash counter, staring at its owner. Jiten Bhai stares back, then consciously looks away. The radio isn't giving up, still gazing in the same direction. Finally, Jiten Bhai gives in. The main knob is turned clockwise.

India are reeling at 111 for 5. Make that 111 for 6. Nelson – the unlucky figure of triple one, signifying the three stumps – has claimed another victim. Kirti Azad is out for a duck to Andy Roberts. Things have gone horribly wrong in the last few overs. The Indians have lost four wickets for 21 runs. They are guilty of throwing away their wickets trying to play expansive strokes. Including Kapil Dev. The captain got carried away by his own hypothesis of scoring heavily against the part-time spinners. Having already hit two boundaries off a benevolent Gomes, Kapil attempted a 6. Only to be caught at long on for 15.

Yajurvindra has had enough. He's off for a day of sightseeing in London, he lets his mates Rajdeep and Jitu know. Whatever little chance India had of upsetting the World Champions is over, he reckons. Like Yajurvindra, Sachin, sitting thousands of miles away, has also lost interest. The 10-year-old cricket enthusiast is more keen to listen to the radio commentary of a third-round match in Wimbledon, featuring his favourite sportsman, John McEnroe.

Jiten Bhai is quick to turn off the radio. Pooja has walked into the shop, catching her father unawares. A sheepish smile is all he can offer as an explanation. Not that his daughter demands one. She reciprocates with a Mona Lisa smile of her own. Enigmatic to most, but not to her father. He has seen this before. He knows what this means. She has something up her sleeve. As it turns out, she does. Literally. Pulling out a piece of paper, tucked inside her rolled-up sleeve, Pooja grabs hold of her father's right arm and places the white slip in his palm. It's a ticket for the finals. There wasn't a musical recital at the neighbourhood, after all. The 16-year-old had gone to Lord's to source a ticket for her father. Gavaskar's early dismissal had resulted in a few fans walking out prematurely. One amongst them was happy to part with his ticket gratuitously. 'Go, Papa, there are still plenty of overs to go.' No more words are exchanged between them. Just a warm hug that lasts seven seconds. Jiten Bhai picks up his coat and walks out. 'Don't worry, I'll manage the shop,' shouts Pooja from behind. He waves his hand in acknowledgement, but doesn't look back. Silent tears are rolling down his cheeks.

India are 161 for 9 in the 45th over when Jiten Bhai finds himself a seat in the open-air stand, square of the wicket, vacated by an Indian spectator who has quit on his team. The stadium, though, is still packed to the rafters as last man, Balwinder Singh Sandhu, walks to the crease where Malcolm Marshall awaits.

First ball, by arguably the quickest bowler in the world, hits Sandhu bang in the middle of his helmet. His red patka, peeking from just inside his helmet, serving as the proverbial muleta to a raging bull. The tailender bent his body back to escape the blow, but the sharply rising missile followed him. Nothing a number 11 and his limited batting technique could do. Sandhu is still on his feet. But his head is spinning. There are a few in the Indian dressing room who understand exactly how Sandhu is feeling. Dilip Vengsarkar amongst them, as he sits in the balcony watching the proceedings. Marshall stands at the end of his follow through, not bothering to inquire about the batsman's well-being, and instead pretends to tie his own shoelaces, in a gesture of mockery. 'I can't think that's the right way to play the game of cricket,' observes the TV commentator. Wicketkeeper Jeff Dujon comes running over, places a hand on Sandhu's shoulder, and asks him how he feels. Sandhu shakes his head. Doesn't say a word. There is obvious pluck in his gesture. Umpire Dickie Bird isn't amused with Marshall's nasty ploy, and orders him to apologize. An arrogant wave of the hand is all the batsman gets from the fiery bowler.

Next ball, Sandhu stands his ground, and whips it towards long on. The following 3 runs receive a louder roar from the crowd than any boundary hit so far. That shot being the perfect embodiment of the Indian spirit on display in the tournament so far. A tournament that's now just an innings away from its ending.

India are all out for 183. Richie Benaud on mic, sums up the Indian effort perfectly: 'India have committed the greatest sin in limited-overs cricket – to be bowled out before the completion of their allotted quota of 60 overs.'

Ayaz, sitting in the press box, can't help but let his journalistic instincts take over. They tell him that India have been dismissed at the exact same juncture at which they finished their semi-final against England. Down to the very ball. The fourth ball of the 54th over. 'Could this be propitious?' But he brushes away the silly thought even before it can plant itself in his head.

Joel Garner can't seem to ignore the outlandish thought that occupies his mind. So, he lets it out. 'Do you think you'll have to bat today?' the West Indian no. 10 asks the no. 8, Marshall, as they walk towards their dressing room. Marshall's reply is even more peculiar. 'Yes, and you will have to too.' Garner's eyebrows knit together instantly in surprise. Even though he started this odd conversation, this wasn't the answer he was expecting. Especially after the way the Indian innings crumbled. Sensing the confusion in his mate's mind, Marshall offers a straightforward explanation. 'When we chase small totals, everybody looks to the next person to finish the job.' Garner finds merit in Marshall's well-argued premonition. 'In that case, we've got a problem,' he concludes.

Michael Holding doesn't share the same pessimism as his two fast-bowling partners. Three World Cups, three wins, is the only thought on his mind as he climbs up the stairs and heads straight into the dining hall to grab a well-deserved lunch.

Holding has reasons enough to be this cocksure. India's 183 is the lowest total in any World Cup final. And the lowest target that the West Indies have been set this whole tournament.

But this lowly 183 is enough to instil confidence in Kapil Dev. 'Boys, as I said at start of match, this pitch is 70 per cent bowling and 30 per cent batting. In 30 per cent, we have 183 on board, but these people still need 183.' The inspiring words from the skipper get a few shouts of 'buck up, boys' and a couple of stray claps from a team that has largely skipped lunch after the poor display with the bat.

As Kapil's Devils walk out after the 45-minute break, Gundappa Viswanath, an inherently happy-go-lucky character, sits dead serious in the balcony, in anticipation of what is to come. A few steps behind him, in the central hall of the Indian dressing room, another former India test player, Syed Abid Ali is kneeling on a white sheet of cloth, praying to the almighty for a miracle. The 42-year-old erstwhile all-rounder knows a thing or two about upsets on the cricket field. Twelve years ago, in the same city, at a ground not too far away from Lord's, he square cut Brian Luckhurst to the boundary and helped India register its first-ever test series win on English soil.

20

Act Three
The Prestige

The Indian team walks out to jeers and jibes from the hostile, predominantly West Indian crowd. The taunts are largely ignored. Except by Gavaskar. A revered figure in the West Indies, he's indulging the partisan crowd, conversing with them in their patois, with a Trinidadian accent to boost, practised and mastered during his numerous trips to the island. His poise and wit today is only adding to his already large fan base in the Caribbean.

It was in the Caribbean that Sandhu lived one of his most special moments on the cricket field. Getting both Haynes and Greenidge – the finest opening partnership in the world – in quick succession during the first innings of the Port of Spain test, only three months ago. Greenidge's dismissal was special. Sandhu got the ball to jag back sharply after pitching and it dislodged the master batsman's stumps. Now, once again, he finds Greenidge at the other end. Once again, he's tempted to bowl an inswinger. But the end from which he is bowling is conducive to outswingers. Thanks largely to Lord's famous slope. And that's exactly why the Indian new ball bowler has *only* been bowling outswingers so far. Plus, the words of his skipper last evening are ringing in his head: 'Oye, sardar, concentrate on outswing. Only outswingers get you wickets at the international level.' Sandhu runs in with ball in hand, the seam facing the on-side. Greenidge is facing the 12th ball of his innings. But this time he chooses not to face it at all. Expecting another outswinger, he shoulders arms to a ball pitched outside off stump, allowing the well-deceived inswinger to kiss his off stump. Sandhu defied his skipper, but the ball obeyed the sardar's orders. The death rattle of leather hitting wood is followed by a chain of expletives from the star opener. Directed at himself. Could it be the batsman's maroon cap, the proverbial red rag, that angered the patka-wearing raging bull? Maybe, Malcolm Marshall can answer that.

There are a few slack jaws in the audience. Murmurs of 'the ball hitting a pebble on the pitch' are floating around. Rajdeep is gloating. 'He's my friend, he's my friend,' he's yelling in joy. It's a personal victory for him. Sandhu is his cricketing buddy. Just a few months ago, they were playing in Bombay's famous monsoon tournament, the Kanga league. Boundaries hit off

Sandhu's genial medium pace are still fresh in his mind. And today, watching his 'friend' do so well at the highest level is in a lot of ways assuring for this budding professional cricketer.

In Bombay, accomplished gully cricketers – Sachin Tendulkar, Avinash Gowariker, Harshad Kulkarni and Ketan Mazumdar – have broken into an impromptu jig watching the Greenidge dismissal. Even before their unsynchronized gyration can come to a halt, Doordarshan, the national broadcaster, has switched to its pre-scheduled programmes of news bulletins and self-help features for farmers.

Haynes is farming the strike. Playing the supporting role perfectly, allowing his more destructive partner, Viv Richards, to take more of the strike.

India is listening to the radio.

Sandhu, this time, is listening to his skipper. Kapil's instructions are clear. 'Keep an eye on where Sandeep is fielding. If he is standing at fine leg, you bowl outswingers. If he is at third man, you bowl inswingers.' On being asked the reason behind this bizarre directive, Kapil has a ready explanation: 'If the ball goes to Sandeep, he will misfield and we will lose the match.' Patil is standing at third man. Sandhu, diligently, bowls an inswinger. Viv whips, the ball using the distinct Stuart Surridge bat in his hands – with the trademark SS sticker on the front – and pulls the ball towards square leg. The leather cherry, made by Dukes for over 223 years, runs along the ground and comes to rest only after hitting an advertisement hoarding beyond the boundary. The billboard reads Red Stripe, written in red over a white background. Its purpose is to hard sell a brand of Jamaican beer. And Viv is contributing immensely to the cause. With their hero on song, the West Indian section of the ground is grooving to live calypso beats. Plenty of lager is flowing in the stands. And Jamaican, Trinidadian and Barbadian flags are flying high, along with a few Rastafarian ones.

Mintu and friends, in their own little way, are also making a contribution. Helping finish off a keg or two. Match situation be damned.

Now, Kapil bowls his preferred outswinger. The batsman takes a step down the pitch, left leg across the stumps, nullifying the swing, leans into his drive, his left elbow – with a white bandage on it – upright, and collects 4 runs straight down the ground. Kapil comes back again. The ball hits the same good-length spot on the pitch. But, swings in. It's the same forward and across movement by the batsman. And it's the same result: 4. Towards square leg this time.

Kapil wipes the sweat off his forehead. Viv hasn't broken a sweat. The Adonis lookalike, one hand on hip, the other holding his bat that rests on his shoulders, is chewing gum, nonchalantly; waiting to deal with the next ball that comes his way. The Australian tearaway fast bowler Dennis Lillee is sitting in the West Indian player's balcony, enjoying every moment of Viv's craftsmanship.

Madan Lal is brought into the attack. The West Indian vice captain greets him with three boundaries in one over. All three have travelled to different parts of the field: midwicket, extra cover and point. All done with the minimum amount of risk, speeding across the turf, straight out of a batting handbook.

A shopping guidebook is called upon by the Indian players' wives. Watching from the stands, they've had enough. The dangerous Viv Richards is 30*. Gavaskar's better half, Marshneil, calls out to Sandeep Patil, who is fielding at third man, closest to them. 'We are off to Oxford Street. Just tell Sunil to meet me at the Wood Green station in a couple of hours. I'm sure we'll be done with our shopping and he with the match by then.' Marshneil, Annu Lal and Romi Dev are off. The gatekeeper at the exit does his bit by warning them: 'Re-entry isn't allowed on these tickets, ma'am, once out, there's no coming back.' The ladies don't entertain a second thought. They aren't too sold on watching a one-sided match.

In India, those keen on watching, still can't. The pre scheduled news bulletin is over, but the live microwave link is down. Mohammed Rafi, dressed in a suit, singing his evergreen hits at a previously recorded concert, is serving as a filler for the national broadcaster. The radio informs:

Desmond Haynes is out for 13. Clive Lloyd is walking out to a standing ovation, presumably because this is his last match as captain. There is something strange about his walk. He seems to be holding his hamstring, spasmodically.

Madan Lal has claimed Haynes, and now wants to have a go at Viv Richards. Kapil isn't too keen. Viv feasted on Madan's last over. The captain realizes he needs to arrest the flow of runs or the game is done. 'Maddi pa, you take a break. I'll get you back after a few overs.' Madan Lal has India's first one-day win against the West Indies on his mind, achieved just three months ago. 'Kaps, give me the ball. I got Viv in Berbice, I'll get him here too. Just one more over, please.' The conviction that whenever the great Vivian Alexander Richards is in good flow, he is also the most vulnerable is what's driving him. Kapil gives in.

The tie-and-jacket-clad Rafi on TV is crooning his hit from the 1961 blockbuster *Hum Dono*, starring Dev Anand. Madan Lal comes into bowl to Viv Richards, batting on 33 off just 28 balls. '*Main zindagi ka saath nibhata chala gaya* – I kept giving life company,' says the first line of the song. The ball is dropped short. Viv rocks back and pulls it with utter disregard, as the next line of the song plays out: '*Main fikr ko dhuen mein udata chala gaya* – I kept blowing away every speck of worry in rings of smoke.' The ball has travelled miles up in the air. Perhaps not connecting with the full face of the master's bat. Then the next line of the song comes along – '*Main fikr ko dhuen mein* uda...' – similar to the line before, but with a long, pregnant pause at the end.

Time stands still at Lord's. Yashpal, at deep square leg, is closer to the ball, and is making a dash for it. Kapil, a natural athlete, stationed at midwicket, has turned around and is also chasing the skier. His instincts dominating his mind at the moment. Patil, at third man, is thanking the almighty that he isn't standing where Kapil was, else he would have been expected to run. Kapil, running backwards, covering quick distance with his limber, long strides, has the ball in his line of sight. Before he can stretch his hands out to attempt the catch, he sees Yashpal from the corner of his eye. 'Yash, don't; it's mine!' he screams. Yashpal slows down in his tracks. After a 20-yard sprint, Kapil has grabbed what seems like an unimaginable catch. The stadium has erupted. The entire team is running towards their skipper to celebrate. So are a bunch of Indian fans who have invaded the ground. The next verse of the song plays out on Indian TV, '*Barbadiyon ka jashn manata chala gaya* – I kept celebrating, even failures'.

Viv Richards: caught Dev, bowled Lal. Mrs Lal and Mrs Dev are out window shopping.

'India must now sense they have a chance,' is how the commentator is assessing the situation. Kapil doesn't share the same optimism, yet. Larry Gomes has been dismissed soon after Richards. The West Indies are 66 for 4. But Kapil knows Lloyd is the key. His counterpart in the West Indian team has the reputation of turning matches on its head. Like in the 1975 World Cup final. His innings of 102 is part of cricketing folklore. This time though, the situation seems different. The burly left-hander is looking distinctly uncomfortable, clutching his hamstring, and is unable to stretch and make full use of his long reach. Desmond Haynes is doing the running for him.

The TV link in India is up and running.

Roger Binny comes running in. Just a ball before, the skipper, standing at mid-off, had a piece of advice for his medium-pacer: 'Lloyd can't move, so don't bowl short to him. Bowl full and force him to stretch.'

Effectively on one leg, Lloyd is out of his depth. Controlling a full-fledged off drive does prove to be a bit of a stretch.

Ambling off the ground, the sun-hatted, moustachioed, bespectacled West Indian skipper looks more a doctor than a sportsman. But it's Kapil who has got his prognosis right. What's more, it's Kapil himself who accepted the catch with glee, flashing a smile more contagious than the one after Viv's dismissal. This is also the first time that panic has set in amongst the West Indian faithful. Sitting in their midst, Rajdeep can sense it. For them, Lloyd, the 'Supercat', stands for all that's stable.

There's a cat among the Indians too – Srikkanth, the idiomatic cat on a hot tin roof. Bacchus's is the 6th wicket to fall. The West Indies are hurting at 76 for 6. Kirmani is hurting too. He's had the ever-hyper Srikkanth, celebrating the fall of Bacchus's wicket, jump on his shoe with his spikes on, leading to a bleeding foot: a reward of sorts for the fantastic catch the wicketkeeper has taken.

The Indian dressing room is flooded with all and sundry. BCCI officials and their friends have barged in, sensing victory. What better place to celebrate than the players' room.

India need four wickets, West Indies 108 runs. Sandhu bowling. Kapil shouting instructions from mid-on after every ball. Jeff Dujon and Malcolm Marshall are adding some important runs to the board. They're playing each ball on its merit.

Dujon whacks a short-pitched ball for 6 over square leg. The West Indian 100 comes up on the old, manual scoreboard. The subdued Caribbean crowd comes alive. Kapil is feeling the nerves. His instructions to the bowler have now mutated into imprecations – spelt out in chaste Punjabi. Sandhu isn't pleased. He complains to the vice captain. Amarnath intervenes, sends Kapil to square leg and stands in his place instead.

But the game isn't changing. A quick single here, a streaky double there, and the 7th-wicket partnership has got the

West Indies within 76 runs of the target. Kapil's anxiety levels are spiking. Every few deliveries he can be heard screaming, '*Judd jaao, jawaano* – Come together, soldiers' in an effort to inspire his 10 men on the field.

The three others – Shastri, Vengsarkar and Valson – reserves for this game, can't bear to watch. They reckon the uninvited party that has bulldozed their way into the dressing room has brought them bad luck. 'Boss, ask these people to leave; else we will lose,' they ask Man Singh to do the needful. But the team manager can't help them. Dictating anything to the BCCI officials is above his pay grade.

Keeping up with Indian superstitions, Jitu and Rajdeep have decided to leave their seats and walk along the periphery of the ground. Mintu and friends aren't leaving their seats. They've had a pint too many to be able to walk straight. Jiten Bhai hasn't left his seat since he entered the ground. Not when Viv was caught, nor when Lloyd fell. A man of phlegmatic temperament, just being able to watch his team play a World Cup final is contentment.

Dujon and Marshall seem content picking up easy runs. Just 65 needed off 114 balls now. An emergency meeting is convened. The team's think tank – Gavaskar, Kapil and Amarnath – come together in the middle of the ground. The BCCI officials have dispersed. They're back in their VIP seats. Gavaskar reckons Amarnath deserves another over or two. 'He's been inexpensive; I think they aren't finding him the easiest to play,' is the Little Master's rationale.

On cue, Amarnath bowls a sedate, innocuous-looking delivery. The ball pitches outside the line of the off stump. Dujon, at first, wants to play it. Then he wants to leave it. He can't do either. The ball hasn't reached him. When it eventually does, he chooses to leave it. A decision, taken after a fair amount of indecision, has resulted in a deflection off his bat. So agitated is Dujon watching his stumps disturbed that he's slapping the ground with his bat, well aware of a third world title slipping away from the Windies's grasp.

The death knell rings in the last ball of the 52nd over. Michael Holding, caught plumb in front, off Amarnath. Umpire Dick Bird has his finger up in a flash. The West Indies have fallen 43 runs short. Pandemonium follows! Crowds invade the ground, Rajdeep and Jitu amongst them.

Amarnath runs and picks up a stump. Dickie Bird picks one up too. Not as memorabilia, it's serving as his weapon to chase away the swarming fans running on to the centre of the pitch. Gavaskar has pocketed the ball and is running the fastest he ever has, towards the safe confines of the dressing room. They are all running. The magnitude of their achievement, yet to sink in.

David Frith swallows his pride. The *Wisden* editor gets up from his seat in the press box, raises his right arm in acknowledgement of underestimating the Indians, and, with his left hand, makes a gesture of eating his words. Ayaz stands up and applauds. The rest of the room follows suit.

'Kapil, the Curry King', reads a poster in the stands.

The curry king of Southall, Mintu Bhatia, is emotional. Standing on the ground, arms around his friends Saran's and Kulwant's shoulders, gazing at their heroes waving to them from the dressing-room balcony, they are slurring their way through their favourite song, '*Yeh dosti, hum nahi chodenge* – We'll never part with this friendship'.

Inches away from them stands Rajdeep. The just-turned 18-year-old is sipping a beer. Not bought, but discovered. Thrown on to the field by a disgruntled West Indian fan. Half already had.

Half a sip is what the Indian players are getting. There aren't enough champagne bottles in the dressing room. Kapil brought the only one. Smuggled in his bag. Quietly confident of causing an upset.

More than a few upset faces sit in the opposition dressing room. That hasn't deterred Kapil from walking in, and requesting for the chilled bucket of champagne lying there. Lloyd lets him take it.

In the VIP stands is a certain Sir Gary Sobers. Hordes of fans are seeking his autograph. 'Not today, this is India's day,' he tells them.

The day is over in India, but the night is still young. Sachin and Co. are dancing away on the streets of Bombay.

The Test and County Cricket Board, the organizers of the tournament, has finally sent across half a dozen bottles of bubbly to the Indian dressing room. But with over 100 people packed in – from board members and their friends, to friends of players, to random fans – a sip or two is all one is getting at best.

Clive Lloyd, the losing captain, is asked for his opinion. 'Indian cricket has arrived. And it's here to stay.'

Kapil Dev holds the trophy aloft. At the Home of Cricket. His mind flooded with thoughts. The controversy over the captaincy... The team selection drama... The worst-possible warm-up... The put-down by the pundits... The resurrection against Zimbabwe... The misunderstanding with Gavaskar... The snub by the hosts... The miracle at Lord's... The Miracle at Lord's!

Jiten Bhai has left the stadium. Overflowing with unbridled joy. His feet moving briskly, guiding him to his shop. Not ready to celebrate yet. Not until he can embrace his daughter. The pink-coloured ticket, crumpled, letters printed in black, held tightly in his closed fist: Win: India; Odds: 66:1.

Epilogue

'Kapil's Men Turn the World Upside Down', read a newspaper headline the morning after. 'The Bewitching Hour When an Indian Legend Was born', said another.

Wisden Cricket Monthly, in an act of self-deprecation, printed a picture of its editor, David Frith, the following month, eating the scathing article it printed against India, sporting a regretful grin on his face.

Ayaz stayed on in England for a few more days as a tourist. Soaking in the sights and sounds of what was then the sporting capital of the world, London. Everywhere he went, from the hallowed turf of Wimbledon, to the Wembley stadium – all steeped in history – he was referred to as being from the country of the Cricket World Champions. Gandhi, evidently, had been pushed to no. 2 on India's list of brand ambassadors. Ayaz would later go on to become one of the leading cricket journalists and columnists in India, rising to be sports editor at the largest English newspaper in the world, the *Times of India*. After four decades of writing on sports and covering various historical events – such as the 'Race of the Century', featuring Ben Johnson and Carl Lewis; the 1988 Seoul Olympics; Michael Stich upsetting Boris Becker at Wimbledon in 1991; Sunil Gavaskar's farewell test knock against Pakistan in 1987; V.V.S. Laxman's 281, arguably the greatest test knock by an Indian batsman – Ayaz maintains that India winning the 1983 World Cup remains the most gratifying sporting event he has ever seen.

The day after India lifted the World Cup was even more special for Mintu Bhatia than 25 June 1983. Harry reported to work at his father's restaurant, wanting to learn the ropes of his family's business. He walked in without his English pals by his side, but with a turban on his head. Fourteen years later, in 1997, the Southall train station got a signage with the Gurmukhi script. Harry, along with a group of other Indian expats, had lobbied for it.

Jiten Bhai claimed his jackpot from the bookmakers the day after the final. A total of 39,600 pounds. Pooja joined private piano lessons and graduated from the Royal Academy of Music in London a few years later. The proud father ensured that only his daughter's recordings were played on the speakers installed in all three of his newly opened shops across London.

Rajdeep pursued his cricketing dreams, playing university-level cricket in both India and England. But he never managed to emulate his father and play for the country. His true calling would be journalism. Over the years, he emerged as one of the leading political analysts in India and one of the most recognizable faces on Indian TV.

Denied extra passes for the final at Lord's, and smarting from the discourteous attitude shown by the English organizers, BCCI chief N.K.P. Salve met his Pakistani counterpart, Air Marshal Nur Khan, the next day for lunch in London. Hurt at the high-handedness shown by the self-appointed potentates of the game, Salve, a central minister, floated the idea of taking the World Cup away from England's clutches. Not one to take an insult lying down, he convinced the then prime minister Indira Gandhi and industrialist Dhirubhai Ambani to offer full support to his plan. The Indo-Pak joint bid guaranteed to pay every participating country 50 per cent more than what they had received in 1983. The English cricket establishment could not match this bid financially. As a result, the other full and associate member countries voted in favour of the 1987 World Cup being held jointly in India and Pakistan.

The Indian team arrived to a grand welcome at home. Between 50–60,000 fans turned up at the Bombay airport.

Thousands more watched, lining the streets on both sides, as the victory bus parade marched from the airport to the Wankhede stadium, where a public reception was organized. Kapil sat next to the driver's seat with garlands around his neck. The rest of the team sat in the lower part of the double-decker bus. Overenthusiastic fans threw soft-drink cans at them, some performed *aarti* on the sidewalks. A journey that would usually take an hour, took four hours that day. Upon reaching the stadium, Sandeep Patil was asked by a journalist about the secret of their success. 'Kapil always gave us instructions in English, which we didn't understand; so we did what we felt like, that's how we won,' was his tongue-in-cheek reply.

The Indian team collectively won 20,000 pounds in prize money. Sandeep Patil, Yashpal Sharma, Kapil Dev and Roger Binny each earned an extra 200 pounds for winning Man of the Match awards. Mohinder Amarnath pocketed an extra 1,000 pounds on two occasions, the semi-final and final, when he won the Man of the Match awards. Some players received a year's supply of pulses from a food company. Mohan Meakin, one of the country's largest breweries, announced the supply of beer for an entire year. The cash-strapped BCCI offered a reward of 2,00,000 rupees to the entire team, which amounted to roughly 14,000 per player. To which Sunil Gavaskar is reported to have responded, 'We are not asking for tips, sir.' The Indian cricket board then set about organizing a fundraising concert, featuring the popular Bollywood singer Lata Mangeshkar, who agreed to do it for free. The cultural programme was held in New Delhi and saw the entire squad hum a line or two on stage. Eventually, each member received 1,00,000 rupees from the proceeds. Days later, Pranab Mukherjee, the finance minister in the central government led by Indira Gandhi, mooted a proposal that the prize money given to the World Cup winners be exempted from taxes. The proposal was accepted by the Union Cabinet as a way of thanking the cricketers on behalf of a grateful nation.

The 1983 World Cup win got Sachin Tendulkar madly hooked to cricket. Exactly nine months after, Ajit Tendulkar, having seen his younger brother's prodigious talent from close quarters, took Sachin to one of Bombay's most-renowned cricket coaches, Ramakant Achrekar. The rest, as they say, is history.

Tunbridge Wells never hosted another international match.

The Clive Lloyd–led West Indies came to India a few months after their defeat at Lord's. Retribution on their mind. The tour dubbed as the 'Revenge Series' saw the visitors winning the tests 3-0 and the five-match one-days 5-zilch.

Acknowledgements

Writing this book not only helped me relive one of the finest hours in Indian sport, it also proved to be an exercise in patience and perseverance – virtues that are in short supply amongst TV journalists. Blame the nature of our work where every few days a 'breaking news' pops up, and the ones that we have worked on so passionately till then are consigned to the pages – or tapes in this case – of our ever-increasing archives, only to be called on as references once in a few years. Spending six months with the same story and characters resuscitated those senses that had eroded after 17 years in TV news.

I'm eternally grateful to Kapil Dev, Sunil Gavaskar, Madan Lal, Yashpal Sharma and Kirti Azad, members of the 1983 World Cup winning team, for their time and for being so forthcoming with their thoughts and memories from the tournament. You sirs, along with the rest of the team, were my first sporting heroes and remain an inspiration till date.

A very special thanks to Sachin Tendulkar for opening up to me about what the 1983 World Cup win meant to him, and how it ignited a passion that was to see him become the greatest cricketers of his generation.

Thanks to Ayaz Memon and Rajdeep Sardesai for sharing their insights and experiences of having witnessed this momentous event from such close quarters. I've had the pleasure of knowing them both for many years, and they've been two seniors I have always looked up to, ever since I became a sports journalist.

Apart from interviewing some of the players, I have also relied on a few other sources: *The Devil's Pack: The Men behind the '83 Victory*, by Balwinder Singh Sandhu; *Sunny Days: Sunil Gavaskar's Own Story*; *Victory Insight: A Manager's Diary for the 1983 and 1987 World Cup*, by P.R. Man Singh; *Marshall Arts: The Autobiography of Malcolm Marshall*; and ESPNcricinfo scorecards and the match report by John Ward.

None of this would have been possible without the support of my family. My Wife, Rupali, well aware of my tendency to procrastinate, kept pushing me to write and even took over my responsibilities around the house just so I could finish this book. Naisha, my daughter, barged into my study ever so often, demanding that I play with her than type on the computer;

her good-natured obtrusions worked like a charm in relieving me of stress. My biggest supporter – my mother, Tripat, for her confidence in me, for believing that I was good enough to narrate this story, more than I believed in it myself.

To my literary agent, Suhail Mathur, a young boy matured beyond his age. I will never forget our first meeting at the Noida Golf Club, when he tried to convince me to write a book on cricket based on my experiences of having covered the game all across the globe. But when I said that the 1983 World Cup was the story closest to my heart, I remember his being excited and convinced about the idea instantly. That enthusiasm is what eventually led me to finish this book.

Last but not the least, the team at Hachette: Poulomi Chatterjee for having faith in me and the story (of course, her being a cricket fan helped), and for being generous and understanding when I missed my deadlines. Cibani Premkumar for being the best editor one could ask for, and for being ever so patient with my errors and demands. Many thanks to Shanuj V.C. and Jyotsna Raman as well for their editorial inputs.